MW00572848

Mobile Vending

Mobile

Vending

How To Run A Traveling
Food Or Merchandise Concession
(Version 2 – Revised and updated)

By Jarvis Hooten

Mobile Vending – How To Run A Traveling Food Or
Merchandise Concession (Version 2 – revised and updated)
– By Jarvis Hooten

Copyright © 2020 – Night Owl Ink – All rights reserved.
No part of this publication may be reproduced or distributed
without prior permission of the publisher, except for brief
quotations embodied in critical reviews and certain other
noncommercial uses permitted by copyright law.

Night Owl Ink Publishing
1661 Tonantzin Place, El Paso, TX 79911

NightOwlInk.com

Information in this book is intended for advisory purposes
only. Use of any information is purely the option of the
reader. No warranty of results is offered or implied. Starting
a business involves risk. Author and publisher of this book
are not responsible for any losses incurred by readers.

All images were captured or created by the author and edited
by the author.

ISBN, EBook: 978-1-7350426-0-2
ISBN, Paperback Book: 978-1-7350426-1-9
ISBN, Hardcover Book: 978-1-7350426-2-6
ISBN, AudioBook: 978-1-7350426-3-3

US Copyright: 1-8814019451
Library of Congress Control Number: 2020908742

Mobile Vending – Contents

Reno Wings Cook-Off

1 Deciding If This Business Is Right For You

"Do What You Love..."

One of the things I like best about the mobile vending business is it allows me to pack my work into several months of the year and then have a few months of the year completely free. Folks who choose mobile vending as their home-owned businesses work extra hard during festival season, then have lots of time off in the fall and winter. Many of us complain about how busy we are during the Christmas season, especially in the retail industry. Wouldn't it be nice not to have any job at all during the whole month of December?

We're going to start with a somewhat philosophical look at owning a business. Every successful venture begins with a successful state of mind, so that's the place to begin this guide. We'll dive into the nuts and bolts of mobile vending shortly.

There's a wonderful old story about a hardware store owner who went to Mexico on vacation. One afternoon he stopped into a small pottery shop, where he found an attractive pot that he thought would look nice in his store back home. He bought the pot for five dollars and packed it away in his suitcase.

Back home in the States, our hardware store owner unpacked his hand made pot and set it on a shelf in his shop, planning to find a plant to put in it the next day. Within hours after opening his store for business, one of his customers noticed the lovely pot and asked about buying it.

"Oh, the pot isn't for sale, actually," the shop owner explained. "I got that in Mexico as a decoration for the store."

As the day went on more customers asked about buying the pot. The shop owner kept explaining the pot was a decoration and was not for sale. After all, the hardware store owner reasoned to himself, he was not in the pottery business. Finally, one customer came out with an offer that was too good to pass up. "It's just what I've been looking for!" the customer said. "I'll give you fifty dollars for it."

The shop owner realized he had happened onto a hit product. He made another trip to Mexico and returned to the small pottery shop. He told the elderly owner he wanted to buy a hundred more of those pots, perhaps in different sizes and colors, and asked how much the potter would charge.

The old Mexican potter thought for a moment, then said, "For that many pots ees twenty dollars each."

"Twenty dollars?" the shop owner responded in surprise. "But that's four times as much as you charged for just one." He tried to explain to the potter that, in business, the price for an item should go down when sold in large quantities.

"Señor," the Mexican potter smiled, "One pot, ees fun. One hundred pots, ees work!"

This old story has two important lessons. The main lesson is obvious: Anything, even your favorite activity, can become a chore when you *have* to do it repeatedly. The wise Mexican potter understood crafting one item as a hobby is fun. Crafting a hundred items as your means for income is work.

A person who enjoys gardening might think it's fun to grow five or six tomato plants in their back yard. Growing tomato plants is a whole different thing for a farmer who has five or six hundred acres of them.

Once you go into business doing something, you'll begin doing it because you have to, not just when you want to. Perhaps you love to bake or you're a hobbyist who enjoys woodworking. Will you enjoy baking or crafting the same things over and over, hundreds of times? How will you feel when those items you put your heart and soul into meet the scrutiny of customers?

The old expression "Do what you love and the money will follow" is true, but it's not the whole story. Yes, of course, you'll be more successful in business or a career if you pursue something you enjoy doing. But when the thing you love to do becomes the thing you do for an income, the thing you love becomes your job. There will be times when you won't love doing it but still have to do it.

Also, when people are paying you to do that thing you love, whether they are your customers or your employer, they get to have a say in how you do it. No one, no matter how glamorous their life may seem or how enjoyable their work may appear, gets to make a living doing *only* what they love all the time. Even over-paid movie stars have to do things they don't enjoy. There are some elements to every business and every vocation that aren't fun.

Here's the philosophical point: To succeed at running your own business, you need to enjoy the *business* of being in business first, then choose the kind of business you want to pursue. Your passion for your craft won't carry a business unless you also love marketing, planning, supervising, taking responsibility, and customer service. It also requires gumption and raw nerve to take charge of your income and, for that matter, your life.

The other, less obvious lesson to the story is: Be flexible. You have to sell what customers want to buy, and what they want may surprise you. If your ideas of fantastic, fun products don't sell, and customers repeatedly ask for something else, be

Jarvis Hooten

prepared to sell something else or go out of business.

A chef from Norway might make the best lutefisk in all of Scandinavia. But he'd have a hard time selling it at a Cinco De Mayo festival in Arizona.

If you're reading this and are excited about starting your own business – because you'd love to work your own *business*, not because you think it would be fun to do your craft all day – then you have the right personality to succeed. This is true for any business you may want to pursue. Now let's look specifically at what you may like or dislike about the mobile vending business.

Mobile Vendors Have To Be, You Know, Mobile!

The factors that make mobile vending fun to some are the same factors that make it miserable to others. Topping that list is the very nature of being mobile. Traveling vendors have to construct their shops for each event, then destruct their shops at the end of each event. They often have to stay in hotels or RVs. Every event has a different environment, different hours and different people to adjust to.

Some folks need consistency in their lives. They want to go to work at the same time and same place every day. I'm not going to say setting up my stand and taking it down are my favorite tasks. (Here's proof that no one gets to do only what they love all the time.) But traveling and being in different environments for each event are among the things I like most about mobile vending.

This merchandise vendor was at a flee market, so the sloppy set-up was almost expected. It would look awful at a crafts fair.

Being a mobile vendor also means going where the people are, which usually means going to fairs and festivals. If you live in central Montana or northern Maine, your travel expenses to festivals will be so high your opportunities will be limited.

Having your home in a remote part of the country does not mean mobile vending is completely unworkable. You could set up shop at parks on weekends where hundreds of kids play soccer and bring along their soccer parents. Some mobile vendors enjoy surprising success setting up in shopping center parking lots, and, of course, there are those familiar sandwich wagons that visit construction sites every day.

So you don't have to go to fairs and festivals to make money, but fairs and festivals are usually where the money is made in mobile vending. A park with hundreds of soccer kids and parents can't compete with a festival attended by tens of thousands of people. To participate in those lucrative festivals without suffering ridiculous travel times and expenses, you need to live in or near populated areas where the festivals are held.

Event Organizers – Good, Bad, And Ugly

Imagine a fixed location store and mobile vendor with the exact same line of products, same customer service; everything about the two shops is the same, except one is permanently located in a shopping center, the other sets up temporarily at festivals. Traffic to the fixed store is dependent on location and advertising. Traffic to the mobile vendor at a festival is dependent on traffic to the festival itself. If an event is poorly attended or poorly organized or has bad weather, the vendors suffer.

There is a fairly new outdoor mall in Reno called The Summit Shopping Center. The stores are laid out in such a way that customers can park right in front of any store and enter the store directly. Shoppers aren't required to stroll past several stores to reach the store where they intend to shop.

It's quite satisfying as a vendor to have an adorable little girl say, "Thank you very much!" as she can't take her wide eyes off the treat her Mom let her buy.

Dozens of small, unknown shops have failed miserably at The Summit. It's gloomy to walk around that mall and see so many available spaces; spaces that once held stores that were the hopes and dreams of small entrepreneurs. Meanwhile, highly recognized stores enjoy wondrous success. That mall is home to Reno's only Apple Store. At one time there was a kids' clothing store right next to the Apple Store. The kids' clothing store failed within months. While it was open, the clothing store was often completely empty while the Apple Store was bustling with business.

You could open a shop in a mall and make a success of it, even if the mall is failing. That's provided you have something like an Apple Store with a highly popular product, extremely devoted customers, and you're the only store of its kind in town. Wait, you don't have a store like that? Do you have an inexhaustible advertising budget? Can you operate at a loss for a few years until your unique product catches on? Hmmm, maybe mobile vending is a better option.

At a well attended festival, even completely new vendors do well, if they have reasonably good set-ups and products. The flip side is, if a festival is failing, mobile vendors can do nothing to improve their sales. People will not go to a festival just to visit one vendor, as they might go to a mall just to visit one store.

A mobile vendor relies on events for facilities. Some event promoters provide vendors ample electrical power, water, trash removal, and easy access to the grounds. Other event organizers are happy to collect vendor fees and then forget all about the vendors' needs.

The answer to these problems is simple. Don't go to failing festivals run by lousy organizers! Of course, the problem with that is you won't know who the lousy organizers are at first. Some people who get into mobile vending quit after a few bad experiences. With a little perseverance and research you'll learn who to do business with. You'll also learn what to look for and how to weed out the bad events.

The mobile vendor advantage on this factor is cost. Fixed location stores have more control over their traffic and facilities, but at good events, mobile vendors have access to throngs of customers at a fraction of the cost of the fixed location shop. What a nice way to segue into the next factor:

Start Up Cost

Starting up your own business for the first time is like buying your first house. You just can't believe all the unexpected expenses involved. Sorry to be the one to tell you this, but starting a mobile vending business comes with plenty of those dreaded unexpected costs. Still, compared to the expense of starting up a fixed location business, mobile vending is a bargain.

What's more, mobile vending is less risky to start than a regular shop. Fixed locations have fixed costs. If things aren't going as planned, a "brick-and-mortar" store can't close for a few months then start up again. Well, it could, but not without continuing to incur huge expenses.

Beautifully designed concession units like this are built by several manufacturers; can be on trailers or trucks. They can be be entirely self contained with onboard generators and plumbing, so they can do business anywhere with no hook-ups. Such elegance comes with a price. A trailer like this costs over $100,000 new.

As a mobile vendor, you could start out doing just a few events a year while continuing to work a regular job. If you run low on capital, put your equipment in storage until you've saved up the cash you need to resume doing business (my experience exactly). If you lose money at an event that was poorly organized, you have the option not to go back to that event. Mobile vendors can completely change their menu or products without having to rebuild their customer base. A fixed location store has none of this flexibility.Here's the way a friend of mine explained how to anticipate the costs of starting any business: Make a list of all the expenses you expect to incur in the first year. That includes all equipment you need to buy, all inventory and advertising – not just for your first month or two but for an entire year. Estimate the cost of retail space rental (in our case this would be vendor fees), vehicles, fuel, maintenance, licenses, insurance, employees, office supplies, postage, printing, tools, cash register, display cases..., every possible expense you can think of. Don't use bargain prices on this stuff. Pretend you are buying everything new, even if you plan to seek out deals on eBay or CraigsList.

Okay, got your grand total? It's a pretty scary number, isn't it? Now double it. That's how much you'll need to start your business.

Ouch! Wait, what about the stories of multi-millionaires who started up their businesses with just a few hundred bucks? Yep, some folks are extraordinarily lucky. Some folks win lotteries, and some people leave Las Vegas richer than when they arrived.

The harsh truth is about half of all new businesses fail in the first three years, and, in almost every case, it's because they run out of money. Don't be discouraged. This is one of the advantages to mobile vending. You don't have to come up with all that capital before you even get started, as you would if you were opening a fixed position store or restaurant. A mobile vending business can be started part time and built up gradually. It's a fun business for couples to do together (provided they get along in the first place) or even get the whole family involved.

Long Days Of Work, Long Days To Play

Here's another factor that I find very attractive about mobile vending, while others find it dreadful. During an event we mobile vendors work long hours, and those hours change from one event to the next. If you're like me, you'll find working events to be fun and stimulating. Every sale is a few more dollars in the bank. Thousands of people are _paying_ to be at events, while I'm _making_ money at events. I take in the same sights and sounds as the paying attendees, listen to the same bands, watch the same entertainment, but I'm earning an income the whole time. That's a bonus to me. Still, it takes plenty of stamina to keep your energy up for twelve or fourteen hours, then come back and do it again the next day.

The pay-off comes when we're not working an event. Each long day of business earns us two or three days of leisure. Mobile vendors work very hard, long hours for a few days, then enjoy the luxury of lots of free days. If you prefer a steady, evenly paced schedule, you may not make it as a mobile vendor. On the other hand, if you like packing your work into intense portions of the year and then having entire months off to do other things, this is the business for you.

When The Going Gets Tough, The Tough Go Vending

Almost all events you'll work as a mobile vendor will be outdoors. You'll be under a tent or canopy, of course, and you may have a trailer with air conditioning, once you can afford it, but you'll still need to endure a lot of exposure to the elements. Working a mobile vending stand requires long hours on your feet, plus bending, reaching, and lifting. Some mobile vendors I know keep working well into their 70's, so it isn't too terribly hard, but you need to be aware that this business strains the body.

Before you work your first event, it's beneficial to do a bit of physical training to get prepared. A couple weeks before the event, start taking long walks, go to the zoo and don't sit down the whole time you're there, do a few knee bends every day, stand in place and pass a heavy jar back and forth between your hands. You get the idea. These kinds of activities will help prepare you for the physical demands of your vending business.

I recommend having stools to sit on from time to time. Stools allow you to get off your feet but keep you at eye level with customers. Sitting down low on a regular chair makes you appear to be on break, out of circulation.

Festival vending – it ain't for sissies!

Staffing Your Stand –
Harder For Mobile Vendors

As we just covered, many people want to be in businesses with steady hours and consistent conditions. This is even more true for employees. It is very difficult to find a quality, reliable worker who is willing and available to tend a vendor booth three days one week, two days the next week, not work at all for three weeks, then show up for four days another week. There are high school and college age kids who are happy with a little summer income and don't require a steady schedule. However, even the best of those young ideal employees may not be available or willing to travel. And if they do go along to an out of town event, that adds lodging them to your expenses.

The need for temporary employees is so common that some event organizers have a hiring day to assist vendors. They advertise locally that vendors will be hiring workers for an upcoming event and set a date and time, usually just before the event starts, when vendors and potential employees can get together.

It is also common for job seeking people just to show up at the start of an event and walk around asking vendors if they need help. To my surprise, some vendors actually rely on finding workers this way. I'm not trusting enough to hire someone literally right off the street.

The difficulty with finding employees is why mobile vending is perfect for couples – the ideal "Mom and Pop" business. This assumes, of course, that Mom and Pop get along and can work with each other. Couples with teenage kids can make a fun family business of mobile vending, provided again those teenage kids get along with each other.

Eventually, though, you'll want your Mom and Pop business to grow and be capable of handling large, fast paced events. Putting your teenage, well behaved kids to work in your stand is nice, until they get older and start careers of their own. That means you need to think about hiring people. Since the thing we're discussing is whether or not mobile vending is the right business for you, you need to be aware that hiring people for mobile vending is often more complicated than hiring staff for a fixed position business.

My solution to this dilemma came when I discovered the wonderful world of temp agencies. Of course, like you, I'd known of temp agencies before. My "discovery" was how well they serve employers like us mobile vendors.

Kelly Services and Manpower are the most well known and are my favorites to deal with. They do the screening and hiring for me. They choose the best qualified person or persons from their pool and send them to my booth. It's terrific. I do have to pay more to hire someone through an agency than hiring them directly, but I'm perfectly happy to do that and save myself a lot of hassle.

Temp agencies are particularly helpful when you do out of town events. Just hop on the old Internet (Heh, who would have thought twenty years ago that we'd ever refer to it as the "old" Internet?) to find the Kelly Services or temp agency of your choice in the town you're going to, and give them a call. They'll want to know the kind of work you are hiring for and the hours you need it done – usually there is a four hour minimum – and they'll arrange your temp worker, just like that!

There is one catch to using temp agencies, but it has an easy work-around. Generally, temp agencies need to set up a billing account with an employer. This requires a rather hefty amount of advance paperwork, a credit check, and time for approval. The work-around is simply to pay the agency in advance. That eliminates their concern over whether or not they will be paid, which is why they create billing accounts in the first place.

I've had two failures with temporary agencies. One snobby agency told me flatly they didn't offer temp workers for food service jobs. Another wanted to charge me the ridiculous rate of $22 an hour per worker.

Another way some traveling concessionaires find workers is through civic and charity organizations. They make arrangements to give a portion of sales to civic groups in exchange for members of the groups working theirs stands.

At Cherry Creek Arts Festival in Denver, Colorado, Coors staffed its beer tents with people from a variety of civic groups. Beer tappers were volunteers from the local public television station and other organizations.

At the Best In The West Rib Cook-Off in Reno, Nevada, an ice cream company had several freezer carts located throughout the festival grounds. The carts were cleverly staffed with cheerleaders from a local high school. This seemed genius to me. The cheerleaders were, in a word, *cheerful*. They were cute as they could be in their cheerleader outfits. And customers liked knowing a portion of their purchases would help send the girls to a cheerleading competition.

Trouble with using volunteers to staff a stand is – they're volunteers. They are not being paid, and they are not working directly for the concessionaire. This can lead to problems with reliability and discipline. The cute cheerleaders selling ice cream were terrific, until I came across one who was being a typical teenager. Perhaps she'd had an argument with her boyfriend, or her parents had scolded her. She was pouting, looking at her phone constantly, and not greeting anyone who walked by. The poor girl was not having a good day. In her youth and immaturity, she projected her displeasure onto everyone else. If that had been my ice cream cart, I would have been displeased, too.

Ready To Get Started?

Okay, we've covered the basic advantages and disadvantages of a mobile vending business to a fixed position business. Mobile vending is less expensive and less risky to start up and run, but it's also less consistent and less predictable than a fixed position store. You'll work hard, long days at mobile vending but have long periods of free time.

Mobile vendors need the stamina to work outside in a variety of weather conditions, spend many hours on their feet, and they need the flexibility to travel to events. Hiring workers for mobile vending operations is more complicated than for other businesses, but those complications can be overcome with a little planning and preparation.

That's about it. Those are the main factors that make mobile vending different from running a regular shop location. Still want to give this business a try? Great! Now let's decide what kind of vendor you want to be.

This lady offers hand crafted jewelry. Customers can suggest designs, and she'll custom craft them on the spot.

2 Food Or Merchandise?

Y ou likely already have an idea of the kind of shop you want to start and the kind of products you want to sell. However, you may not realize how much the two kinds of vending differ and the advantages and disadvantages between them. We just compared mobile vending to fixed position retail businesses. Now it's time to compare food vending to merchandise vending.

Merchandise Vending

Merchandise vending is easier than food vending and, aside from the initial investment in stock, which, if you are a crafter making your own items, would be a large investment of time, it's less expensive. Almost all events charge merchandise vendors a lower booth space fee than they charge food vendors. I'll get to the reasons for that when we discuss food vending.

Merchandise vendors draw far less scrutiny from government agencies than food vendors. Let's face it, unless you're selling weapons or chemicals, neither of which is likely to be allowed at any event other than a gun show, merchandise poses little risk to public safety. Merchandisers don't use propane stoves or other devices that create fire dangers. Merchandisers don't sell prepared foods that could create public health risks. Fire departments and health departments don't give merchandise vendors a second glance. In most cases, the only two government documents a merchandise vendor needs are a business license and a sales tax permit.

If you are a crafter, or you know a crafter whose products you'd like to sell, this decision is already made for you. Be a merchandiser. That is, of course, provided the crafted products you want to sell are things people want to buy! That may seem obvious, but there are plenty of folks who invest mountains of time and money in merchandise businesses before first being sure their merchandise would sell.

Whether or not your cool doodads or amazing gizmos will sell is difficult to predict. Some items defy all logic and sell like crazy. (Anyone old enough to remember Pet Rocks?) Other items seem to be sure sellers, but end up falling flat.

Do a little research. Visit a few festivals and see what other merchandisers are selling. A wonderful resource for researching merchandise is that good old Internet again. Check eBay and Etsy and other online selling sites to see what kind of collectibles, trinkets, and curios are being offered.

This impressive contraption is a coin stamper. The steel weight is hoisted up by the pulley, then drops with a powerful – and LOUD – impact on a coin at the base. I don't know how profitable this stand is, but it sure drew attention.

That brings up another advantage to merchandise over food; you can sell merchandise online! Hey, maybe you should just skip the mobile vending idea and go straight to opening an Internet shop. Bad idea. Online stores are almost impossible to get off the ground without huge investments in advertising and expensive web design.

Selling merchandise online is easier to get started if you already have a mobile vending shop. People who visit your booth at a festival might like an item but not quite be in the buying state of mind. Make sure everyone who leaves your booth takes with them your business card, which has your web site address. You might print an "Online Special Discount" coupon on the back of your cards.

If you've done your research and feel confident your selected merchandise will sell, you still need to be flexible and be prepared to make changes according to customer demand. As I mentioned in the first chapter, you may pour your heart and soul into crafting your items, only to find those items snubbed by picky customers.

Don't let your feelings or your confidence get hurt. Your art is still wondrous and exquisite in its own way. Your family still loves you. But you will have to adjust your craft to satisfy your customers. Or you could just quit the business and do something else for a living. The world isn't ready for your art. That's fine, but it means you are putting the fondness for your craft ahead of your desire to run a business.

Let's say you are a wood carver, and you love dogs. You have an idea to sell darling hand carved Christmas ornaments in a variety of dog shapes. You work for months carving ornament after ornament until you have enough inventory to open shop at your first festival.

Surprise! It's *cat* lovers who are more likely to buy animal themed trinkets than dog lovers. Don't believe me? Visit the home of a dog lover, then visit the home of a cat lover. See whose house has more dog or cat themed bath towels, coffee mugs, door mats, hot pads, wall hangings, and so on.

Being a hobbiest is fun. Making money with a hobby is even funner!

Phooey! All that work in dog-shaped carved wood, and customers keep asking if you have any cat-shaped stuff. Are you upset? Of course, but only a little. There are still dog lovers who will eventually buy your dog shaped ornaments. If you truly think like a business person, though, you're excited to have found out what really sells!

Merchandisers outnumber food vendors at most festivals. Event organizers often have no limit for merchandisers, while they tightly restrict the number of lemonade stands, barbecue joints, and Kettle Korn booths. Some events go so far as to have two separate organizers for managing merchandisers and food. At the Best In The West Rib Cook Off in Reno, merchandise vendors go through one organizer, pay a ridiculously low fee, and have no trouble getting into the event. Food vendors, on the other hand, have to go through the main sponsor of the event, which is The Nugget Casino. It can take years for a food vendor to get into the Rib Cook Off, and they have to pay a whopping thirty percent of their gross to The Nugget.

The final advantage to merchandise over food, and it's a big advantage, is merchandise is non perishable. A wood crafter can hang on to the dog shaped ornaments that didn't sell at one event and put them back up for sale at the next event. There are some items food vendors can keep in their inventories, such as cups and other paper products. But perishable items that don't sell have to be thrown away, or those leftovers are what food vendors eat themselves for the next month or give away to friends, not items they can sell at future events.

The non perishable nature of merchandise also means inventories can be stocked up well in advance. Food vendors have to stock their perishables right before every event – sometimes daily during an event. Merchandise vendors can find a good deal on their products and buy up a whole season's worth ahead of time.

Food Vending

Gosh, with all those advantages to merchandise vending, why would anyone choose to be a food vendor? Oh, that's easy: MONEY! Food vendors almost always make more money than merchandise vendors. In that case, why does anyone choose to be a merchandiser? Because food vendors <u>earn</u> their higher payoff. Food vending is considerably more demanding than merchandise vending.

Let's examine some advantages to food vending first. Aside from the big obvious advantage of making more money, food vendors have less inventory to keep track of. Yes, they have to stock up more often, since they are dealing with perishables, but a food vendor's full menu is almost always shorter than a merchandise vendor's full line of products. A merchandiser might carry a couple hundred items, while a food vendor should only have about a dozen items on his menu.

Food vendors also have the luxury of not needing to contend with "tire kickers." Those are the browsing customers who take up a vendor's time by "just looking." There is the occasional picky food customer who wants a free taste sample of an item, then says, "Not what I want," and walks away without making a purchase. Those customers are rare. Almost everyone who goes to a food booth, especially if they have to stand in line for a while, is there to make a purchase.

Wowsers, this is one helluva barbecue stand! Lots of color, pictures and razzle-dazzle. This complete rig cost a quarter million dollars or more. It required six people to operate and took up eight 10 X 10 vendor spaces. At good events they do $10,000 *per day*. But imagine the painful expense of a rained out day!

The disadvantages to food vending are generally the inverse to the advantages of merchandise vending. For starters, almost all events charge food booths higher fees, often much higher fees, than merchandise booths. When I first learned this, I thought it was unfair. Then I looked at it from the event organizer's point of view.

Food booths generate many times more trash and require much more electrical power than merchandisers. Food booths have to have access to waste water tanks and grease dumps; services a merchandiser does not need at all.

Food booths bring along inherent risks that merchandisers don't have. Even the most conscientious food vendor might accidentally sell some tainted food, making dozens of people sick. A food vendor's deep fryer might tip over in a strong wind and burn someone or cause a fire. The food vendor at fault would have to take responsibility and would face the ensuing law suits, which is why food vendors are required to carry liability insurance, but event organizers might also be held accountable for allowing the faulty food vendor into the event in the first place.

A food booth requires a rather hefty investment in equipment. While merchandisers just need display tables and racks, food vendors usually need expensive commercial cooking equipment, refrigerators and freezers, fryers, and hot holding devices. Some ideal food stands don't require much equipment at all, and we'll discuss those, but generally, a food vendor can expect to spend more start-up money on equipment than a merchandise vendor.

If you're reading this book, you probably already know the type of booth you want to run. Some folks just love merchandising while others love food service. If that's you, and you know what kind of vending you enjoy, wonderful. The decision is already made. Merchandisers and food vendors can both make good money in the mobile vending business. If this were not true, there would not be plenty of both merchandise and food booths at every festival. Still, I thought it would be beneficial to point out the advantages and disadvantages of the two vending types.

Saw this concession trailer at Reno Rockabilly Riot. The trailer was practically new - interior was immaculate, and they made fantastic pizza. But the guys were standing around waiting for customers. Their sales were slow because their trailer LOOKED so boring and uninviting. Just one big "PIZZA" banner and some color would have made a huge diference.

3 Let's Get Your Business Started!

What To Sell – Start Simple, Let Customers Tell You What They Want

I clearly remember the moment I first got the idea to start a mobile vending business. It was at the 2001 "Star Spangled Sparks" July 4th celebration in Sparks, Nevada. That was the first time I saw a Kettle Korn stand. Kettle Korn has become a standard at almost all festivals, so it's easy to forget the sweet and salty treat is relatively new to the modern festival food world.

In case you're interested, or, like me, you like to know the true history of things, Kettle Korn is not new at all. It was first popular at festivals in the 1700s. Somehow, it lost its appeal and disappeared almost completely during the 1900s. If you have been to any kind of festival in recent years, I don't have to tell you Kettle Korn is enjoying a huge comeback in the 21st century.

At that July 4th celebration in 2001, I first spotted the Kettle Korn stand from behind. There was a man inside a tent stirring the contents of a giant kettle with what appeared to be a canoe paddle. This immediately captured my attention. It looked as if he were stirring a witch's cauldron from a cartoon. As I watched, the corn started popping and quickly filled the kettle to over flowing. It looked so fascinating I just had to try it. I walked around to the front of the stand and discovered a dozen or more people standing in line to buy this amazing new kind of popcorn.

The lady at the front of the stand was handing out big bags of Kettle Korn, sometimes two or three to a customer, and taking in five dollars for each bag as fast as she could. By the time I reached the front of the line, it occurred to me these folks had made at least $75 in sales in just the five minutes I had stood in line, and by that time there were ten more people in line behind me! The seed was planted. This might be a fun home-based business I could try some day.

A few years later, circumstances became right for me to give mobile vending a try. I looked into starting a Kettle Korn business, but by then the market was flooded with Kettle Korn vendors. It's easy to understand why. Kettle Korn is a dream product for food vendors. It has a huge mark up, immediate recognition by customers, requires only a few ingredients, and the very process of making it draws attention. Kettle Korn also has high perceived value. A customer can buy a gigantic bag of Kettle Korn for about the same price as a single slice of pizza or a barbecue sandwich.

Meet Squeaky The Clown. She was at Tahoe Arts Festival. I was happy to give her any item on my menu for free, and I was happy to tell her why. She became a living, eye-catching advertisement for my products! Be good to fellow vendors, especially the entertainers.

Many vendors pounced on the Kettle Korn business with its renewed popularity in the 2000s. By the time I started trying to get into events, I was told by organizers that I was at least the fourth or fifth Kettle Korn vendor they had heard from. My friend JP Pinocchio, who manages food vendors for Reno Rodeo and Reno Air Races, told me he hears from about *thirty* Kettle Korn vendors every year.

Can you see how important it is <u>not</u> to invest tons of money into your business before you research what to sell? I was very relieved that I had not spent thousands on a Kettle Korn rig before finding out if I could book it into events.

With the industry over-run by Kettle Korn vendors, I decided to try offering nachos, hot dogs and limeade. I happen to make an award winning chile con queso (nacho cheese) sauce. Yes, really, it won an award. Several years ago, at a small chili cook-off in Colorado, I entered my chile con queso in the "Sauces and Dips" category. There were only two other entries in that category, both guacamole, and my queso won easily! So my "Award Winning" brag isn't very impressive, when you know the rest of the story, but it is legitimate.

With my homemade nacho cheese sauce, I figured to have an advantage over the nacho stands using canned nacho cheese sauce. Further, I would offer jumbo hot dogs, not the regular size, and I would roast them instead of boiling them. My beverage would stand out from other stands because it would be limeade, not lemonade. Oh, and I also had coffee makers on hand, which turned out to be a stroke of very good luck.

Those were the products I offered at my first festival and, wonder of wonders, I made money! And that event was rained out the first day. The rain was the reason my coffee makers were good luck. After the rain cleared it was quite chilly outside. All of a sudden, I was selling more coffee than anything else. I was the only vendor offering a hot beverage.

I could have stayed with that line of products and probably done fine in the vending business. Nachos, hot dogs, and limeade are staples that customers expect to find at all fairs and festivals. A simple line of recognizable products is what I recommend all food vendors start out with for their first season.

The approach is similar for merchandise vendors. If you are crafting your own items, make a small variety of them to start out with. If you are buying merchandise to resell, start out with a short list of products.

Here's what will happen, as it happened to me: Customers will let you know what they want. This will happen both by direct contact with customers and through indirect reference by event organizers and other vendors.

When I was trying to shop my idea of a Kettle Korn stand and was being told by event organizers that they'd already heard from several Kettle Korn vendors, I began asking them what they would like to see. Some organizers gave a dumb response like, "Just something different," but others gave me specific ideas. In particular, one organizer told me she'd like to book a Polynesian food vendor. That small suggestion stuck in my head and is one reason my stand is now called Tropic Hut.

Back to my very first event. A couple customers said they liked my limeade but wondered if I could serve it *blended* with ice. Omigosh, what a great idea! Not only could I blend it with ice, I could toss in bananas and strawberries and offer a truly unique blended delight!

Since coffee worked out so well at that first event I decided to make it a permanent part of my menu. Later in that first season I was at an event in Incline Village, Nevada, on the north shore of Lake Tahoe. It was a particularly warm day in the mountains, so coffee was not selling much, except to hardcore java junkies. A girl stepped up to my stand and said she loved coffee, but, with it being such a warm day, she wondered if I would mind serving it over ice.

Iced coffee! Of course! How had I not thought of it? Not only could I offer iced coffee, but by then I had added blenders to my equipment. I could make *blended* coffee drinks!

See what happened? I started out selling nachos, hot dogs, and limeade. Within just the first few events, my whole product line changed. Blended tropical and coffee drinks, neither of which was remotely among my ideas when I started my business, became my biggest money-makers. I have not sold nachos or hot dogs at all in years.

Start simple, let customers guide your options.

Jarvis Hooten

Oh, I know, you have visions of your hand crafted figurines becoming popular across the nation and filling shelves at Walmart. You believe your recipe for pizza rolls will be the next big thing in festival food. You want to buy loads of equipment and expensive display cases to unveil your dream products.

My first stand at my first festival. Only sign I had was a small menu board. At least I hung Christmas lights for some color. I built and put up a wood fence in front in keeping with my theme and booth name - "Crunch Corral."

Slow down. I hope your dream products work out exactly as you envision and you enjoy phenomenal success. Really, that would be terrific. It would also be very, very rare. It is much more likely that, in order to stay in business and enjoy any success at all, you will have to adjust your vision a bit as you see what customers and event organizers want.

Read the stories of successful companies. In almost every case, big companies do things very differently from what the founders started out doing. Ivory Soap was invented entirely by accident when a worker left the soap mixer running while he went to lunch, resulting in air being whipped into the batch. This made the finished soap float. Proctor and Gamble had not intended to manufacture floating soap, and they might not to this day, had not so many customers asked for more of the newfangled floating bath bar. It was sheer accidental luck that gave them a hit product. Thomas Edison was actually trying to invent the world's first telephone answering machine when he accidentally created the phonograph. Steve Jobs and Steve Wozniak, founders of Apple Computer and considered the two greatest visionaries of the computer age, had no idea they were changing the world when they invented the personal computer. It was an investor with boatloads of cash who saw their potential and gave those two kids the money to start Apple Computer.

It's okay to have a grand dream for your business. Yes, it's important to have some kind of plan to start out with. The point here is not to let your grand dream or plan get in the way of real opportunities.

Your objective at this stage of the game is just to get in the game. Get started. Do your first events. Do not spend a bunch of money or time on equipment, a custom tent or trailer, exotic signage, an elaborate web site or any novelty advertising products. Do not try to start out with a huge menu or catalog of products. There will be plenty of time (and, let's hope, money) in your second and third seasons to acquire all the glorious trimmings you dream of for your business.

This wood crafter added just a couple simple decorations to his stand to make it much more appealing. The poster in the background and rug on the ground give the booth the look of a cozy cabin. Both decorations are easy to transport.

All you really need for your first events are a tent, service and display tables, the basic equipment necessary to make your short list of products, some good but inexpensive signage, and a cash box. If you can afford a trailer, that's great, but do not go crazy customizing it in your first season.

If your experience is like mine, you will begin discovering new ideas and thinking of improvements to your products right from your very first event. Here's the tricky part: By the time you do your first event, you will likely have already sent applications to several other events. Do not spring new products on those future events without first checking with the organizers. Vendors who show up at events intending to sell products that were not in their applications create conflict with other vendors and make themselves very unpopular with event organizers.

Simply contact the event organizer and explain you have come up with a new menu item or line of merchandise. Describe your new item and ask if it would be a problem for you to offer it at the upcoming event. Make it clear you are perfectly happy to sell only the items you were already accepted to sell. For some events, changing your product line is no problem. For others, it is a major issue.

As I described earlier, I came up with the idea of blending my limeade drink at my very first event. It did not occur to me that blending my drinks put me into an altogether different vendor category, so I didn't mention it to other events to which I had been accepted. Come to find out, using a blender made me a smoothy vendor, not just a beverage vendor, and other smoothy vendors can be very obstinate about competition.

Attractive, compact mini-donut stand.

A few weeks after my first event I introduced my new blended drink at Tahoe Arts Festival. It was a terrific success and created no issues with other vendors. At that small event there were no other drink *or* smoothy vendors, so there was no one to complain. Two weeks later I was at Reno/Tahoe Blues Fest. Before the event even started, a smoothy vendor noticed my blended beverage sign and raised a big stink. The event organizer informed me I needed to take down that sign and completely remove my blenders from the grounds, or I would not be allowed to sell at the event.

If you come up with a change to one of your products that is really subtle, it probably won't be a problem. You could change the kind of cheese or pickles you use for your hamburgers without creating a conflict. However, if you started out with beef hamburgers and decided to add buffalo burgers to your menu, that's a big enough change to justify clearing it with event organizers. It would be lousy to spend hundreds of dollars on ground buffalo, only to have the "exotic" meats vendor forbid you to sell a single burger. After all, that other vendor spent hundreds on ground buffalo, too, and that's been one of his feature products for ten years. You wouldn't want to try to compete with him, anyway.

If you carry gold plated jewelry and decide to add solid gold pieces, that would be okay. But get it cleared first if you add a line of turquoise jewelry to your catalog. There may be a jewelry vendor from Santa Fe who carries nothing but turquoise and may have been guaranteed exclusivity.

Remember, I thought upgrading my drinks by simply offering a blended variety wouldn't be a big deal. After all, it was still a tropical fruit drink, just blended. What's the problem with that? Turned out it was a big problem.

Here's a funny follow-up to the story of the other smoothy vendor at Reno/Tahoe Blues Fest: I have since done several events where that vendor was also booked. He turns out to be an okay fellow, aside from being a bit demanding. Several times in recent years I got my applications sent in to events before he sent in his applications. That meant I got to be the one to tell *him* whether or not he could sell smoothies. I'm not a demanding jerk, so I didn't disallow his use of a blender. I had seen his stand and was not worried about his competition. Sure enough, at every event where he and I have both been selling smoothies, I have beat him soundly in sales. Nyuck, nyuck. No wonder he doesn't like competition!

The popularity of your items will help you decide which products to build up and which ones to drop, but be careful not to be too hasty in your decisions. You may introduce a new item that seems to go over great the first time you offer it, but then hardly sells at all for the next five events. Or a new item may seem to be a flop for several events, then sell like crazy at the next events. My stand has real world experience of both these possibilities.

After introducing Tropic Kabobs to my menu and finding them to be successful over several events, I decided to try adding an "up sell" item to go with the kabobs. For a dollar more, customers could get a bowl of rice with their pork or beef kabob. Rice has a very low food cost, and I figured customers would enjoy the option of getting a much more filling serving of food for just an extra dollar.

Rice may have a low food cost, but adding it to my menu required carrying a bunch more stuff with my stand. I needed to stock the rice itself, of course, plus two rice cookers, utensils for serving the rice, and containers to serve the rice in. All this extra gear took up a lot of precious space in my booth.

The rice sold pretty well at the first event where I offered it. About a third of the customers who bought kabobs also bought the rice. For the next several events, though, only a few folks who bought kabobs also bought rice. It occurred to me I was dragging along lots of extra equipment and stock for something that sold for just a dollar per serving. Even if two hundred customers bought the rice, that's just two hundred bucks increase in sales. The rice wasn't worth the trouble and was taken off my menu.

When I tried adding Chocolate Dipped Frozen Bananas to my menu, the opposite happened. Several events went by with very few customers showing any interest in the frozen treats. I had prepped three food containers full of them and, after five or six events, still had two containers full in the freezer. I decided Chocolate Dipped Frozen Bananas were not going to work, but, since I had two containers of them left, I figured we might as well offer them one last time to see if a few more would sell.

At that last event where we offered Chocolate Dipped Frozen Bananas, both the remaining two containers sold out within hours in the first day.

Customers continued asking for them for the rest of that event. Hey, guess what got put back on the menu! I have discovered that, for some reason, Chocolate Dipped Frozen Bananas are extremely popular at some events and hardly sell at all at other events.

It takes several festivals to decide if an item is going to sell or not. Don't allow yourself to become discouraged or excited about a new product's performance after the first event you offer it.

If you are buying an existing business, you have a strong advantage in choosing your products. The previous owner should have done several seasons ahead of you and found what works and what doesn't. Also, the previous owner should have made lots of useful contacts with event organizers. If you are taking over an existing business, go into your first season doing what the previous owner did. Your first year is not the time to launch all your spectacular ideas for how to improve the business. Incorporate your ideas gradually. Some of your ideas will work wonderfully. Some of your other ideas will make you realize the previous owner knew what he was doing after all.

4 Booking Events: What You'll Need BEFORE You Apply

Business License

Before you make that first phone call or send out that first application, there are a few things you must have. First, get your business license. In most states, before you can even get your business license, you must register your business name. That's if you want your business license to reflect your business name, which is the case for most of us.

If your name is Joe Smith, and you want to call your business "Joe's Barbecue," then you need to register "Joe's Barbecue," even though your first name is part of the business name. Thanks to the wretched terrorist attacks of 9/11/2001, banks and all government agencies have become very stringent about business registration and business licensing. Any time money goes to an entity with an assumed name, government agencies want to know who's behind the assumed name.

To allow yourself some flexibility, you can get a business license under your own name and not have to register an assumed business name. This way Joe Smith is licensed to do business in his given state, and he could still call his stand "Joe's Barbecue." However, he could *not* open a business bank account with the name "Joe's Barbecue," because "Joe Smith" is the name on the business license. Federal laws force banks to be extreme sticklers about opening accounts in assumed names.

This was how I started out – with a state business license in just my name. As a festival vendor, I figured I didn't need a business bank account. No one was going to be buying my products by check, and I was content to pay my vendor fees using my personal bank account.

Then two things happened. An event organizer sent my cleaning deposit back with a check made out to "Tropic Hut," and another event organizer called me to ask why I was using my personal account to pay vendor fees. I could have asked the first event organizer to send me another check made out to my name, but that seemed unprofessional. And it obviously seemed unprofessional to some organizers that I didn't have a business bank account.

To maintain flexibility with your stand name while registering an assumed business name, you could call your business something general, such as "Joe Smith Enterprises" or "Festival Foods" or "Shooting Star Specialties." This way you can change the name of your actual stand, or branch out to have several different stand names, so long as they all operate under the one business license.

In most locations in the United States you only need a state business license to be a mobile vendor. Sometimes a temporary local business license is required to participate at a given event, but that is usually handled for you by the event organizer. You do not need a permanent business license for every county and city that you might take your stand to. That would be crazy expensive.

Dealing with government agencies that handle businesses is not like dealing with the dreaded DMV (Department Of Motor Vehicles, or whatever it's called in your state). Government agencies that handle businesses are usually much more responsive and helpful. Just locate your state's web site and do a little research to see what requirements you need to get a business license. Then, to be sure you're completely covered, find your county's and your city's web sites, and do the same research. Make some phone calls, tell them what business you'd like to be in, and see what is required.

These agencies may be better and nicer than the DMV, but they are still government agencies. I've seen forms that required me to fill out my name, business name, and complete contact information twice on the same page. No kidding – not separate pages within the same form, but right there on the same page. Only a government agency could come up with a form as absurd as that.

How cool is this? At The Quartzsite RV Show, I got to set up my stand right next to my trailer. Step inside and I was home. Step outside and I was in business!

Some state governments have easy-to-use web sites with all the forms you need readily available for download. Other states do not. Nevada is a good example. Nevada has a well designed, easy-to-use state web page for the DMV, but nothing for the state's health departments. Nevadans never have to visit a DMV office to renew their vehicle registration or driver's license. They can do it all conveniently online. Nevada businesses can file sales taxes online, too. The health departments are another story. Nowhere in the state can a food business apply for a health permit online. Nevada health permit applications have to be snail-mailed or submitted in person.

I wish I could offer some way to save you from these steps to make your business official. Perhaps you'll find the entire process simple and streamlined in your location, which would be wonderful, and I'd like to know where you live. My prediction is somewhere along the way you will encounter at least one ridiculous snag with a government agency. May it not be too painful.

Sales Tax Permit

The moment your business license is issued, your next step is to apply for a sales tax permit. A business license is usually required to apply for a sales tax permit, so don't try to start this step until you have your business license. Of course, Oregonians get to skip this one, because Oregon has no sales tax. However, if an Oregonian wants to do business in California or Washington, better get sales tax permits for those states!

This is a biggie for a lot of events. Many event organizers won't even talk with you if you don't have a sales tax permit. You can't get a sales tax permit without a business license, and a business license requires an assumed name registration, so you can see how the red tape starts to pile up if you want to travel to several states with your business.

A sales tax permit can take a long time to process in some states. Arizona, for example, has one of the worst systems for sales tax I've seen. For one thing, they call it "Transaction Privilege Tax." What boneheaded government official came up with that laborious name for sales tax? I applied for my Arizona Transaction Privilege Tax Permit in September and did not receive it until late December, almost four months later.

Arizona also has the most ridiculous, lengthy, redundant form for filing sales tax I've ever filled out, but at least they don't require a huge deposit. Nevada requires a shockingly large deposit, based on the anticipated maximum amount of sales a business might do in any given month. This is the kind of unexpected expense business owners have to be prepared for.

Business Liability Insurance

Business Liability Insurance scared the daylights out of me the first time I was asked for it. An event required I show proof of business liability insurance with coverage in the amount of *one million dollars*. Holy cow, I knew how much my car insurance was for a fraction of that liability. How much would business liability insurance cost with coverage for *one million dollars?!*

Jarvis Hooten

What a relief to discover it's nowhere near as expensive as you might expect. I'll gladly give a plug to my agent, John Jasper of Farmer's, who got my Business Liability Insurance with coverage o f *TWO million dollars* for under five hundred bucks a year.

Not all insurance companies offer Business Liability Insurance. If you like the company that insures your car, house, life, or whatever else you have insured, start with them. You want an insurer that offers good service, because event organizers require Business Liability Insurance Certificates with an "Also Insured" clause. These certificates have to come directly from the insurer.

This isn't like showing your insurance card to a police officer if you get pulled over. You can't just mail a copy of your policy to the event organizer. They require a certificate prepared by your insurer specifically naming the event organizer – and sometimes a paragraph of other parties – as "Also Insured." This certificate must be faxed directly from the insurer to the organizer, so the organizer knows you didn't simply copy and paste the "Also Insured" clause into the document on your computer.

When you build your vending business up and start doing twenty or more events a year, and each of them requires one of these "Also Insured" certificates, you can see how important it is to have an insurance agent who offers good service. With my agent, I send an e-mail with the "Also Insured" clause written out exactly as it appears in the contract. Often I can copy and paste this clause right from their contract, if I have the contract as a computer file. If I only have a paper contract, I type the clause out in an e-mail to my agent. That way he can copy and paste the clause into his own document, which he sends to the underwriting insurance company. The company then approves it and sends the certificate to the event organizer.

Good grief, that's a lot of trouble to show insurance for each event, isn't it? It's not nearly as difficult as it may seem from what you've just read. This is insurance, which means it comes from a private business, not a government agency. If my agent started to let me down consistently, I could just find another agent. Free enterprise beats government every time. Now that I've been doing this for a while, I find requesting Business Liability Insurance Certificates to be a breeze. Good thing, because this is one of the things we mobile vendors must have. Many events will not accept a vendor, particularly a food vendor, who does not have liability insurance.

Special Requirements For Food Service

As you must expect, being a food vendor requires a few additional permits over being a merchandise vendor. None of the special requirements apply until you get your first event booking. But once you get a booking, the very next step is to get your food service permits lined up. Don't allow the fun of securing a booking to distract you from getting permits for that event. I know how it is, especially in your first year. You want to call your friends and share the news. If the event is out of town, you want to check hotels and local suppliers. Try to control your enthusiasm. When an event booking is confirmed, do nothing else until all required permits are lined up. This is usually a step handled by county government offices.

County health departments are generally helpful and responsive to prospective food vendors. They can give you pointers and recommendations on what you'll need before applying for a permit. But they can not issue a permit for a location that does not exist. Food vendors cannot acquire blanket permits for future events they have not booked yet.

One thing a food vendor *can* do ahead of time is become ServSafe certified. ServSafe is a food and beverage safety training program administered by the U.S. National Restaurant Association. The program is accredited by ANSI and the Conference for Food Protection. It has become so well established as the gold standard for food service that many health departments now require ServSafe certification as a prerequisite to open a restaurant. At least one management person must have a ServSafe Certificate at almost all restaurants across the nation.

This may change, but currently most health departments do not require ServSafe certification for mobile food vendors, although it sure impresses them when a food vendor has it. The ServSafe course costs about $125. You can usually take it online, and test administrators can be found in most cities. I took the course and the test in one day. I had the advantage of having worked in food service before, but the course is not terribly difficult.

Whether you have to have certification or not, it's highly advisable for anyone in food service to learn good food handling practices anyway. Might as well get a handsome certificate to show what you know. The ServSafe website has all the info you need:

https://www.servsafe.com/

Menu, Catalog, Photos Of Your Stand

Almost every event you apply to will want to know what you plan to sell. You will stand out tremendously if you create a nice looking menu or catalog *with photos of your actual products*. Oh, I know, this is time consuming and requires some computer skills, but it is so true that a picture is worth a thousand words.

Food vendors should make a sample of each item they intend to sell, take pictures of each sample, and put the pictures with short descriptions into a page that can be sent out with event applications. Be sure to include the size and price of each item in your description.

Product Guide

Tropic Silkie
Real strawberries, banana, brown sugar and milk are *blended* with Topic Twister for a thick, frothy treat! Topped with whipped cream.
20 Ounces: $5.⁰⁰

Java Silkie
Dark Roast Coffee blended with ice, brown sugar, milk and choice of caramel or mocha syrup. Topped with whipped cream.
20 Ounces: $5.⁰⁰

Tropic Twister
Lemon-limeade based drink with pineapple and guava juice, coconut creme and just a hint of mint for a delightful aftertaste.
20 Ounces: $3.⁰⁰

Dark Roast Coffee
Coffee enthusiasts delight! You *can* find rich, fresh brewed, quality coffee at festivals!
16 Ounces Hot: $3.⁰⁰
20 Ounces Iced: $3.⁰⁰

Tea
No powders or premixes here. This is genuine, true brewed tea. Crisp and refreshing.
16 Ounces Hot: $3.⁰⁰
20 Ounces Iced: $3.⁰⁰

Chocolate Dipped Banana
Large bananas are frozen right at their peak ripeness, then *double dipped* in rich chocolate sauce.
$3.⁰⁰

Tropic Kabob - Pork
Half a pound of succulent teriyaki pork, skewered with chunks of pineapple and flash roasted to seal in the flavors.
$4.⁰⁰

Tropic Kabob - Beef
Half a pound of tender teriyaki beef, skewered with slices of onion and flash roasted to seal in the flavors.
$4.⁰⁰

(Tropic Kabobs are optional food items we offer only if space and ample electrical power are available.)

Merchandisers need not put photos of every item they carry in their catalog; just a photo of each *line* of products. If you offer hand crafted birdhouses and bird feeders of various types, colors and sizes, get a good picture of each type of your items. Then use your description of that item to detail the available sizes and colors. Include prices and other options you offer. Can customers have their items shipped? Can they have their items customized? Do you accept credit cards?

If you simply can't make up a sample of each of your items, at least take the time to create well written descriptions of the things you intend to sell.

Later on, as you start doing events, you can take pictures of your products on location at your booth. One way or another, get some photos of what you sell. Merchandisers in particular will usually be required to submit photos of their items with applications.

I have advised you to start small and be prepared to change and add to your product list as you go along. It may seem a lot of trouble to make up menus or catalogs of products that you know are going to change. That's true, so, again, start small. Don't spend hundreds or thousands of dollars on professional photography and graphic design. You can make menus or catalogs right on your own computer that will look plenty good. If you have no computer skills, find a teenage kid to do the layouts for you.

Event organizers will also usually require pictures of your stand with your application. Good grief, if you haven't done an event yet, how can you have pictures of your stand? You have a driveway, don't you? Or back yard or nearby parking lot?

Yes, it's a lot of work and a pain in the neck to set up your entire stand just to take pictures of it, but the effort will pay off. As a new vendor with no track record, event organizers are much more likely to consider you if they can see what your stand looks like.

Set up your stand in your driveway or a nearby parking lot, get in the stand, and have someone take pictures of you smiling and waving. If your spouse is involved in the business, get him or her in the photo, too. Then print up copies of the photo with a nice caption like, "Joe and Barb are ready to treat you to some terrific southern style barbecue!"

Quick Review – What You'll Need BEFORE Applying To Events

The two basic legal documents you'll almost certainly need are: Business License and Sales Tax Permit. In most places, Business Licenses and Sales Tax Permits are handled by the state. In others they are issued by counties, and in some rare cases you'll need both state and county business licenses. The one non-government item you'll likely need, especially if you plan to sell food or offer inflatables or do anything with a remote possibility of a person getting hurt, is Business Liability Insurance.

Those three documents are what event organizers require in order to keep their own licenses and permits. Other permits, such as temporary health and fire, come later after you have been booked to an event.

Then you'll need a menu or catalog, preferably with photos of your actual products, and photos of your stand to finish up your prerequisites. Get your legal paperwork done and photos printed, and you're ready to start submitting applications!

5 Where To Find Festivals

Still Need To Start Small

T he actual doing of events is the fun part. When your stand is all set up and customers are buying your products; when someone takes their first sip of your drink and says, "Mmmm, that's really good!" When a customer buys your trinket and says, "Mom's going to love this!" That's the pay-off. The hard part is getting into events in the first place.

Trying to get your first bookings is like trying to get your first job. It's time consuming, often frustrating work. You'll send e-mails that get no replies and leave phone messages that go unanswered. You can't get the first job without experience and you can't get experience without the first job. A young person fresh out of business college should not expect to start out as senior vice president of a major corporation. Likewise, we vendors should not expect to start our businesses with prime locations at major events.

A crowd like this can overwhelm even highly experienced vendors. Do not attempt such big festivals your first year.

There may be fantastic big events in your area that you can't wait to get your booth into. In fact, attending those events is what inspired you to start your vending business in the first place. Don't make the mistake of trying to get into large, well established events your first year. You will irritate those big event organizers, cause yourself a great deal of unnecessary stress, cost your business big fees that you can't afford so early on, and you'll miss out on vital experience you need before trying to take on huge crowds.

Where do you find events to take your new business? Thank goodness for the wonderful World Wide Web. Just do searches for things like "Georgia Music Festivals" or "Kansas Food Festivals" or "California Crafts Fairs," and you will quickly begin to compile a big list of opportunities.

There are companies and organizations that specifically cater to the festival and mobile vendor industries and yes, they have web sites. Here are a few of my favorites:

• Festivals.com (http://www.festivals.com/): This site has a terrific, easy to search data base of small to large events all over the country.

• International Association Of Fairs And Expositions (http://www.fairsandexpos.com/): One of the leading trade organizations for vendors and event organizers. Their site also has a searchable database of events.

• Festival Network Online (http://festival-net.com/): FNO offers detailed information about events and about the organizers themselves. Other vendors can rate organizers on how easy they are to work with. To take full advantage of FNO you will need to subscribe to their service for around fifty bucks a year.

• National Independent Concessionaires Association (http://www.nicainc.org/): NICA is the leading trade organization for the mobile vending industry. Membership is $125 per year for the the primary, then less for spouses and employees. NICA offers many resources, including Health Insurance options, legal guidance, business tips and a members database. If you join, be sure to put "Member, NICA" on your letterhead and business cards, as this will impress event organizers.

Other resources for finding events include your friends and family and even other vendors. Put the word out to everyone you know: You're in the vending business! Go to events and talk with the vendors, but be careful about this. It's offensive for a newbie to walk up to a veteran vendor and ask, "Know any good events I should apply to?" At the very least, buy something from the vendor first. That's an easy way to make any vendor more friendly. And do not approach vendors for information if they sell the same stuff you plan to sell.

Finding and learning events is considered part of the initiation process for all new vendors. Experienced vendors had to earn this "insider information" through hours of research and years of working festivals. Understandably, they'll be a little irritated by a newb who tries to get access to choice events without putting in the same effort.

When you find an event that looks appealing, but it's not one you are familiar with, do an Internet search for "vendor reviews of [name of event]." That's where veteran vendors are more likely to tell their stories.

Once you've been doing events for a while and start seeing some of the same vendors over and over, you will find them to be very open and helpful. That's because you will have become part of the community, and, if you're smart and a decent person, you will have shown yourself to be open and helpful, too. Next thing you know, other vendors will be suggesting events you should look into. Sweetest of all is when event organizers call *you* with invitations because you were recommended by other vendors.

Let's not get ahead of ourselves. As a new vendor, you must pay your dues and get those first events booked. As I have explained, booking events, especially in your first few seasons, is really the work of this business. In six months you will go through more paper and printer ink than you probably had in the previous six years, just from printing applications, cover letters, and copies of your menu or catalog.

Most fairs and festivals take place during summer months, so the best time to be searching and applying to them is January and February. Some southern states, particularly Arizona and Florida, have festivals in the winter months, and there are plenty of events to be found in spring and fall months, too, so at any time of year you can find opportunities. One great advantage to staying with small events for your first year is smaller events are much less stringent than the big ones about deadlines. You could start your business as late as July and still find several small events to fill out the remainder of your summer.

Try to keep your focus on events that charge less than $200 per day in vendor fees. Keep in mind that the number of people attending an event is not what determines a vendor's potential for customers. It's the *ratio* of people to vendors that matters. Two food vendors at an event attended by 2,000 people will do better than two hundred food vendors at an event attended by 20,000 people. (Ratio of 1 vendor to 1,000 attendees versus 1 vendor to 100 attendees.)

You will find it extremely helpful to keep a record of events you apply to. You may have gathered by now that I'm kind of a computer guy, so I do this with a database. When you start sending out applications, it will become easy to forget which ones you have sent deposits, which you have sent full payments, which ones include electrical power and which ones charge extra for it. Having a record of all this information will save you a lot of headaches and embarrassing phone calls. When events begin accepting you, this record will also keep track of what permits you need to get, which events still need Business Liability Certificates, and things like that.

I call my database "Events-Prospects." Having it on my computer in database format allows me to search any field, change the sort order, set priorities and, coolest of all, use it to send mail merges to multiple recipients. I love this stuff, but you could, of course, keep your record in a spiral notebook. After you've sent out a dozen applications you will begin to appreciate the value of having this information written down, whether it's with a computer or with old fashioned pen and paper.

Even if it's out-dated and politically incorrect, clever signage works if it catches people's attention!

Wow, booking events is a lot of work, isn't it? Yep, this is the hard part of the vending business. It does get easier and, in fact, it starts to become fun, because every application sent is a new prospect for opportunity.

Remember, you could always get a a local permit and set up at a park on weekends for the soccer kids and their parents. You would miss out on the bigger sales opportunities at fairs and festivals, but you'd also avoid having to send out dozens of applications every year.

6 Accepted To An Event – Now What?

Final Permits & Licenses – It Only Took Once

Y ou got your first booking. How exciting! Now what? You're not done with government requirements yet, especially if you are a food vendor. Before you do anything else, find out what permits you'll need and get that paperwork finalized.

It only took once. Here's my story of what can happen if you don't thoroughly check to be sure you have every shred of your required government documentation.

In 2006 I took Tropic Hut to Candy Dance, a remarkably popular event in the tiny town of Genoa, Nevada. Around mid-morning of the first day, a pleasant woman approached my stand, identified herself as the health inspector, and asked to see my Temporary Health Permit.

I reached into my file case and dug around a bit but was having trouble finding the permit. I knew it was in there. It had fallen in between some other papers or something. The pleasant woman noticed I was struggling to find the permit and said, "It's okay if you don't have your permit. I can just issue you a new one."

"Really?" I responded with interest. "So in Genoa you can issue Temporary Health Permits on site?" (This is important news!)

"Oh sure," she replied. "State health inspectors carry permits with them."

By this time I had found my permit anyway. She inspected my stand, found everything to be in order, and went on her way, wishing me lots of success. Wasn't that nice?

Fast forward to 2010. I'm back in Genoa at Old Time Music Festival, a much smaller event than Candy Dance, which turned out to be very fortunate.

I had just finished completely setting up when the health inspector came by. This time it was a young man with an arrogant, self-important air about him. He asked to see my health permit and I requested to have the permit issued on site, as I had been told state health inspectors could do.

"Without a permit you have to shut down and leave the premises," he ordered.

"Wait, what? Last time I was here the lady health inspector told me you could issue permits on site."

"That was wrong," said the unrelenting health inspector. "I know the lady you're referring to, and she's no longer with the Health Department."

"Okay, but she *was* with the Health Department and she specifically told me state inspectors can issue permits on site. Isn't there some kind of work-around? Can't I just pay a fine and know better next time?"

"No," he said, unapologetically. "You may not operate a food stand without first acquiring a permit."

"B-but I drove down here from Reno at five this morning and just finished setting up. How could I know that what a previous state official told me was wrong?" It was beginning to occur to me that, after getting up at 4 AM, driving to Genoa and spending three hours setting up, I was actually going to have to break down, load up, and drive all the way back to Reno without having made a single dollar.

"You may not make any sales at this event," came the flat reply from this jackass health inspector. "You must close your stand and leave the premises immediately."

Try to imagine how embarrassing it was, how utterly dejected we felt, packing up and loading out while the event was starting and other vendors were watching.

What a painful lesson to learn, but I learned it well. Even if a government official – someone who represents the very agency that regulates the thing you are doing – tells you something, if it seems unusual, don't trust that it's true. Check, double check and triple check to be sure you have the documentation you need.

It was very fortunate that, if I did have to learn this lesson, it was at a small, one day event that had only cost fifty bucks in vendor fees.

Here's the real kicker. Just a few weeks later I was at another event under the same state health jurisdiction. (It was the Heart Of Gold Cantaloupe Festival in Fallon. A cantaloupe festival! What fun events we mobile vendors get paid to attend.) The health inspector at this event was a nice, middle-aged fellow who had been with the health department for several years. I asked him about state health inspectors being able to issue permits on site. To my utter amazement, he told me yes, they *could* issue permits on site, but they weren't supposed to. He knew the arrogant inspector who had made me shut down a few weeks earlier and told me that guy was new to the department, so he was doing everything strictly by the book. And he was a small-minded jerk who was impressed with his new power, I thought to myself.

I know it's best to forgive and forget. Holding negative thoughts is bad for my blood pressure. But that Nevada Health Inspector who forced me to shut down deserves the bad karma that's headed his way.

If you can get wrong information from one state official that results in another state official closing your shop down, then yet another state official tells you what the first official said was not wrong after all, how can we little business people hope to get anything right?

That's government, folks, and that's just the way it is. Be glad we're not in socialist Cuba or North Korea. In those countries, governments issue flawed information and then execute people who misunderstand. Bad things happen when petty people are given power.

The good news is it does get easier. Once you learn what the requirements are for the places where you'll do business, filling out the forms and getting the necessary approvals becomes just part of the job. You'll start dealing with the same government people. You'll get to know them and, they'll get to know you.

There are a couple of inspectors in Reno who have checked my stand often enough they don't even do a full inspection when they see me at an event. They simply ask if I've made any menu changes since the last time they saw my stand. If I've added something new, they'll give that item a quick check to be sure I'm using proper holding and serving methods. If there's nothing new they just hand me the inspection slip to sign and go on their merry way. This is my reward for conscientious observance of health department standards.

My story is a warning. Be sure to learn all your permit and code requirements *before* you go to any event in an area you have not worked before. If someone tells you something that doesn't seem right, ask someone else to confirm.

The owner of this eye-catching stand told me he designed and built it himself. The top collapses and it fits on a trailer.

When I first got into the mobile vending business, one of the things I looked forward to was traveling the country, participating in festivals from border to border and coast to coast. I knew the costs of such extensive travel would eat heavily into my profits, but I figured it would be worth it for all the fun adventures I'd be having. To me, mobile vending was a way to get paid for traveling.

I had not anticipated how much government red tape would interfere with the fun and feasibility of traveling with a vending business. It's not like the movie "Chef." You can't drive a food truck across the country, stopping in towns along the way to sell whatever food you feel like cooking that day. I learned it's best to choose a region of the country you like working in, get to know the government requirements of the states, counties, and cities in that region, and stick to those places.

My region of the country is the southwest. I have business licenses and Sales Tax Permits for Nevada, California, Arizona, and New Mexico. Some vendors I've met say they routinely go to eight or ten states in a year. That may or may not be true. (Vendors can be as bad as fishermen and gamblers about stretching the truth!) Covering that much territory means an awful lot of travel expense and permits to keep track of.

Event organizers are good places to start your research on the permits you will need. The good ones will actually send out copies of permit applications in a vendor acceptance packet.

If the event organizer does not have all the permit info you need, then jump on the Internet and start looking up government web sites. Usually, the three types of government agencies that will be regulating you are business, health, and fire departments. A merchandise vendor almost always needs a business license and sales tax permit. Food vendors need those same two, plus temporary health permits. Those documents will be the norm for almost every event you do, but some places will require further permits. Be sure to ask at every step of the way, "Do you know of any other permits I may need?"

At The Quartzsite RV Show in Arizona, my stand was required to have no less than six government permits: 1- Arizona State Business License, 2- Arizona Transaction Privilege Tax Permit (their ridiculous name for sales tax), 3- La Paz County Temporary Business License, 4- Temporary Health Permit, 5- Food Handler's Card (for which I had to take a two hour class), and 6- La Paz County Fire Department Inspection. Oh, and the event organizer required a Business Liability Insurance Certificate.

Get the paperwork done so you can stop worrying about it and get on to the fun stuff!

Jarvis Hooten

7 Designing Your Stand

Prepare For The Elements
– It Only Took Once

W e're about to get to the fun stuff, really we are. But first here's one more "It only took once" tale of woe for you to consider.

In May of 2010 I was invited to participate in Reno Rockabilly Riot at Grand Sierra Resort in Reno. Perhaps I should have been concerned, because the event started on a Friday The 13th.

The first day, Friday, went fine. Sales were not spectacular, but it was a weekday, and the gates didn't open until 2:00 PM. I was new to the whole rockabilly craze. The fad combined the charm of the 1950s with the extremes of "millennials." Imagine girls wearing cute poodle skirts and cotton sweaters – with trampy stiletto heals, fish-net hose, and lots of tattoos and body piercings. Hey, I'm not judging. The attendees were fun, friendly folks, and it was refreshing to see live bands that looked like they stepped right off the Ed Sullivan Show. I simply found it amusing to observe the clash of styles between two distinct generations.

What a great looking popcorn wagon! A concession like this does not need big banners or elaborate signs. The wagon itself IS the signage.

Saturday's weather was a bit chilly and breezy, which probably kept some attendees away from the event, but it wasn't cold or windy enough to cause any worries. It was Saturday night, just as I was closing up shop, when the wind storm that had been predicted began to move into the area. Temperatures dropped and winds picked up dramatically. I strapped down Tropic Hut as best I could and hoped for the best.

Next morning, Sunday (and remember this is mid May), I arrived at the event grounds around 10 AM. Temperature was 38 degrees, winds were blowing pretty hard, and I discovered my sink/cabinet unit had been blown over. That was with *two* full five gallon water containers on it. I got the cabinet righted and started the first pots of coffee brewing.

About twenty minutes later, Mother Nature unleashed her fury. Suddenly the wind gusts jumped to such force that my entire stand was being pushed back against the stand behind mine. Two nice fellows rushed over to help me hang on to my banner frames. The three of us kept the stand from blowing away entirely, but the wind was so strong it *broke off* the PVC pipe frames holding my banners at the top.

Inside my tent a wind gust blew an Air Pot off its perch, sending it crashing to the pavement. A moment later my lovely glass iced tea dispenser met its end; wind blew the entire, *heavy* glass dispenser, containing two gallons of tea, right off the counter. My cash register pedestal toppled. The interlocking supports for my E-Z Up Tent broke and popped apart all around the enclosure. Cups, straws, and sugar packets went flying all over the place.

The cruel winds lasted about an hour before they died down enough for me to pull apart the banner frames, which had broken in many places by then. Winds continued to blow, but not quite as hard. Once the banners had been blown down or shredded, the winds didn't have those broad, flat surfaces to pound against.

Strong wind caused several hundred dollars destruction to my stand at Reno Rockabilly Riot, but I was lucky. Some vendors suffered much worse damage.

My tent was destroyed beyond repair, and I lost several pieces of serving equipment, but I was one of the lucky ones. A ceramic vendor at that same event had two entire display cases blown over, smashing all the enclosed figurines. A clothing vendor watched helplessly as blouses and dresses were blown all over the surrounding area, some of them ending up in the nearby water reservoir.

Mother Nature is a formidable adversary to the mobile vendor. Some weather conditions, like the fifty mile an hour wind gusts my stand took at Reno Rockabilly Riot, are too powerful for any stand to take. Eventually, every vendor will have a tale of destruction to tell. However, you can design your vending booth to handle as much adverse weather as possible.

The first concern, of course, is your tent. (You folks who can afford to start out with a sturdy trailer, bully for you. I'll have notes for you in a bit.) Unless you live in a large enough metropolitan area to have a full-line vendor supply store nearby, you are not likely to find a commercial grade tent or canopy at a local store. These things need to be ordered, so it's back to our pal the Internet.

You can find <u>consumer</u> grade canopies by E-Z UP, Caravan, or perhaps ShelterLogic and Undercover brands at big retail and home improvement stores. Consumer grade canopies usually cost around $150 to $250. Commercial grade canopies cost up to five times as much.

Yikes, do you really need to spend upwards of a thousand bucks just for your tent? No, you can start out with an inexpensive consumer grade tent and be fine for a while. Remember the question is not *if* you will be hit by severe weather, it's *when*.

After my experience at Reno Rockabilly Riot, I told my tale of disaster to all my friends and fellow vendors. They offered their sympathies, then shared their own tales of weather disasters. Every vendor, without exception, that I talked with had suffered weather damage at some point. Eventually, it happens to all of us.

Even my Uncle Jaymes, a ceramic and pottery artist of some renown in the Southwest (http://www.jaymesdudding.com/) told me of an art show he had worked in Wyoming. A freak wind blew through his stand, knocking over four sculptures and causing over five thousand dollars in damage. I have to imagine the pain of his loss was far greater than monetary. It must have been agonizing to watch pieces of art he'd poured his heart into destroyed. Heck, I didn't even know he did art shows till I told him my weather calamity story, only to have him top my story with his own!

Do a little research on the types of tents and canopies available. I'd offer some links, but a simple Internet search for "Vendor Canopies" will yield all the info you need. If you can find a used commercial grade tent for a good price, that would be ideal. I would not recommend buying an expensive custom tent with graphics and signage imprinted on the canvas right off the bat. Remember, you are likely to change your products or even your entire theme after you've been in business a while.

What you put inside your tent will obviously depend on what you sell. Merchandisers will want to find tables, racks or display cases that attractively display their items while also being secure. A tall, ornate pedestal may look terrific for displaying your decorative clocks, but, if that pedestal is easily toppled, you're asking for disaster.

It's wise to consider weather in all aspects of your set up. If your booth space is flexible, you may want to extend your displays out in front of your tent. Some events strictly prohibit extending your space, others are pretty relaxed about it. If you do place displays outside the protection of your tent, set them up in such a way that they can quickly be moved if the weather suddenly changes.

This is a well laid out trailer concession. Order window is in front, pick-up window and condiments table on right. The flaw is their signage, which is awful. Hand written paper signs are taped to front. The yellow billboard at top is cluttered and hard to read from a distance.

It's not just weather that can rupture parts of your stand; the people attending events themselves pose a threat. I mean, you hope to have large crowds of folks walking past your stand, right? With lots of people milling around in tight spaces, someone is going to bump into something.

At a music event I worked, a group of friends was enjoying the tunes and got into a circle dance in front of my stand. Plenty of alcohol had been consumed by that time. A guy and girl tripped over each other's feet and fell right onto my service table. They apologized immediately and nothing was damaged, so we all just laughed about it. If I had been a blown glass vendor and that table had held a bunch of vases, it would not have been so funny.

Special Requirements For Food Service

How many sinks do you think a restaurant is required to have? You folks with experience in food service probably know this one. Folks without food service experience may know how many sinks restaurants need for washing dishes – one each for wash, rinse, and sanitize – but that's only for washing dishes. Restaurants are required to have sinks for several other purposes.

An employee who used chemicals to clean the grill should not wash his hands in one of the sinks being used to wash dishes, right? Now you're thinking like a health department. Install another sink for hand washing.

Where will employees ring out rags and dump out buckets of cleaning liquids? Not in the hand wash sink or any of the dish washing sinks. Add a mop sink. Food prep requires chopping and pealing vegetables, which requires yet another sink. Are you keeping track? That's six sinks, which does not include drain sinks in the floor. Health departments don't allow restaurant drains to have direct connections to sewer lines. Even ice machines have to drain into floor sinks, not into direct connections to sewer lines. This way, if there is a blockage in a sewer line, the drain water will not back up all the way into a sink or ice machine. It will flood out all over the floor, which is disgusting, but it won't end up on anything that might touch food.

Reno Wings Cook-Off, 2010 – Notice almost everyone is holding something they bought or standing in line to buy something. This is a big crowd of *buyers* – a vendor's dream.

Okay, food vendors, try to relax. Fortunately, standards for mobile vendors are not nearly so overwhelming. Several stipulations are taken care of for you by event organizers. The organizers have their own government requirements to meet. Among those are adequate toilet and hand wash facilities, waste water dump tanks, and grease disposal traps.

What a gorgeous hot dog stand! Note attendant inside is wearing chef's uniform and hat, not ragged jeans and t-shirt. Great example of how to do concessions right.

A properly equipped food truck or trailer will have a three compartment dish wash sink and a separate hand wash sink built in. A food vendor using a tent set-up can use three bus tubs as dish wash sinks. A hand wash station can be set up next to the tent. Hand wash stations have to meet very specific standards. They must use a water supply with a "free flowing" spigot. That means it needs to be able to keep flowing without the user holding it open. Paper towels must be secured to a holder of some kind. Drain water must flow into a bucket, not simply splash out onto the ground.

In California, hand wash water has to be heated to above a certain temperature. I've seen food vendors carry coffee pots for only this purpose. Perhaps you are beginning to see how food vendors earn the higher profits they make.

Food vendors have to consider health codes in every aspect of their set ups. Every state is different, so learning this stuff is part of the job of food vending. If you are entering the food service business for the first time, you will likely be surprised by some things you will not be allowed to do. For example, I know of no health department in the country that allows using Sternos for holding hot foods outdoors. The Sterno brand offers separate products for commercial food service. Those familiar little canned flames are for consumer use only.

Commissary Kitchen

If you plan to sell "high risk" foods, which include all meats and fish, most health departments will require you to have a "commissary kitchen." A fully equipped trailer or food truck qualifies as a commissary kitchen. If you are starting out with a simple tent for your stand, and you intend to sell turkey legs or chicken wings, you may have to find a commissary kitchen for your food prep and cold storage.

Where there is a need, free enterprise creates a way to fill it. Commissary kitchens are available to rent in most cities. Vendors can pay a fee for access to a commercially equipped food prep location. However, these can be expensive. All a health department is concerned about is that vendors do food prep in inspected kitchens, not in their homes. In fact, you could do prep in your home kitchen, provided it was equipped with stainless steel counters and all other commercial grade food prep requirements, and it was inspected by the health department.

An inexpensive option is to find a church or doughnut bakery – some place with a commercial kitchen that is not always in use. See if you can make a deal with them to use their kitchen a few days a month for prep and use parts of their freezer and fridge for food storage. This may take a while. Check with your health department. They will immediately know how to advise you when you ask about a "commissary kitchen."

Health departments may be intimidating, and they can be overbearing. Try not to be stressed out by the watchdogs. Food safety benefits both consumers and the food service industry. In my many years of doing this business, I have experienced only two health inspectors and one fire inspector who were real jackasses. The rest were friendly, helpful folks. Overall, health and fire departments exist to help, not hurt, the food service industry. Seek assistance from your local health department before you buy your equipment, and you will generally find them to be very accommodating.

Some right, some wrong: Stand is nicely laid out, colorful and attractive; order girl is very friendly (and also attractive, which is always good for business!). What's wrong is they're trying to do WAY too much – menu is absurdly long, and customers have to wait over ten minutes for their orders.

Fire departments will also get involved with a food vendor's set up, if it uses any kind of open flame or a grease fryer for cooking. I occasionally use a counter top propane stove for heating water at events where I'll be selling a lot of cocoa. A surly fire inspector came along one time and told me I needed a "secured" propane tank. He left without explaining what that was. Great, so I have to buy some kind of special tank? My propane tank looked the same as what other vendors were using.

I walked over to one of the vendors using propane and asked where they got their "secured" propane tank and what was different about it. The lady chuckled and told me "secured" just means the tank needs to be set in a milk crate or tied to a table so that it won't fall over and roll.

Couldn't the fire inspector have just told me that? I walked back to my stand, strapped a bungee cord around the propane tank and attached it to a table leg, and – presto – I had a "secured" propane tank.

For guarding against weather, food vendors want to use dispensers and containers for all loose items. Don't set out unsecured stacks of napkins, cups, or rolls of paper towels. One little gust of wind will send those items flying. Dispensers look better and are more secure.

Designing Your Stand For Fun And Money – Signage And Pizzazz

We started out making your stand sturdy. Now let's make it cool.

Consider all the factors that draw customers to a vending booth: Products, prices, booth location, booth appearance, and signage. Of those five factors, appearance and signage are more important than the other three combined. Of course, if you're selling crummy products for exorbitant prices, a nice looking stand with good signage won't help much.

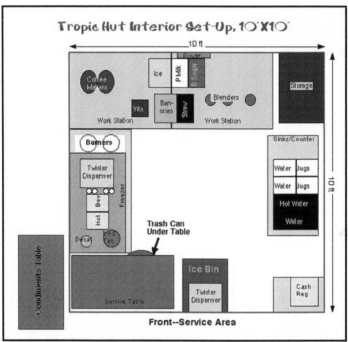

Tropic Hut Interior Set-Up, 10'X10'

Creating this Drawing in OpenOffice was time consuming, but so worth the effort. The exact-to scale images allowed me to work out a perfect arrangement for all the equipment in my stand, right down to cup dispensers. Adjusting these images on my computer was way easier than moving the actual pieces!

On the other hand, a stand that sells average products but has terrific signage will do better than a booth selling fantastic products with poor signage. The effort you put into adding color, decorations and, above all, good signage to your stand will pay off big time in sales.

Most vending booths need two kinds of signage: big banners for far away and small signs for close up. The big banners serve the same purpose for both food and merchandise vendors, which is to catch customers' attention from a distance. The small signage for a food vendor is a menu board; for merchandisers the small signage is price tags on items or groups of items.

It may not look like much here, but this banner frame was among the proudest features of my stand. It precisely fit around the edges of a 10'x10' canopy. The frames across the top were 12.5' high – great for visibility of signs. Conduit pipe was from hardware store, fixtures ordered from online specialty shop.

Many vendors make the mistake of trying to cram too much on their banners. That results in the lettering being small, which defeats the entire purpose of banners. A few descriptive words are good, but you don't want to put your entire menu on one big banner. A single banner that reads "Fresh Baked Stone Oven Gourmet Pizza / Made To Order Toasted Hoagies / Delicious Philly Cheese Steak Sandwiches" is too cluttered. Better would be three separate banners with big letters that read "Gourmet Pizza," "Toasted Hoagies," and "Philly Cheese Steak." Some marketers would recommend simplifying even more with one huge banner featuring your most attractive product in gigantic letters: "PIZZA"

The most effective banners are those that can be read at a glance from at least fifty feet. You want big banners, but an absurdly huge banner with gigantic letters is only useful if it can be seen from a block away, which is rare at festivals. At the other extreme, a small, cluttered banner is easily overlooked.

Having your banners printed is easy and inexpensive, thanks again to our friend the Internet. Do a search for "Banner Printing," and you will find hundreds of companies. This is for your simple starter banners with just lettering and one color printing. Later, I recommend upgrading to full color banners with big photos of your actual products. For those fancy banners I prefer to find a local company, so I can meet with them in person, get proofs of my layouts, and they can keep my designs on file for future printings. Simple banners with one ink color cost around two dollars per square foot. Full color custom banners with photos cost as much as eight dollars per square foot.

Even something as simple as banner printing requires us vendors to educate ourselves. You'll want to be sure what your banner sizes will be *with grommets*. Some unethical banner printers will charge you for a two foot by four foot banner, which is eight square feet, but the finished product is several inches smaller all the way around. They print a banner in the size you requested, then fold over and hem the edges for grommet holes. Sturdy, hemmed edges are good, but not when they reduce banner sizes by half a foot in both width and height. Be sure to specify the finished banner should match the measurements you requested, *including* hems and grommets, and get that in writing.

Printed banners should not show product prices. That's because at some events you will want to change prices. Detailed product descriptions and prices go on a menu board or individual item tags, which can be altered from event to event.

Frames for your banners also can be found online, often from the same companies that print banners. If you're more industrious and handy with tools, you can build your own frames and make them custom fit your booth design. The best materials for banner frames are PVC pipe or electrical conduit pipe, which are available at any home improvement store. If your frames are sim-

Jarvis Hooten

ple rectangles, you'll also find fittings and joints at any home improvement store. For more elaborate PVC frames or for conduit frames, the special fittings are not commonly available at home improvement stores. Those stores usually only carry fittings used in building construction. For banner frame fittings, do an Internet search for "PVC pipe furniture fittings" or "conduit pipe frame fittings."

Hand written signs or price tags make your stand look like a garage sale. If you don't have a printer in your home office, now is the time to get one. Run off a few pages of preprinted price tags on heavy, card-stock paper, cut them into nice rectangles with a paper cutter, and attach those neatly on your items. Food vendors can use menu boards or print up menu pages and laminate them.

Some high-dollar merchandisers argue that price tags are crude or inappropriate for their items. This may be true at a high-priced art gallery or fancy furniture showroom; not so much at an outdoor festival, where most attendees are wearing shorts and sandals.

Other fast talking, pushy peddlers think they can sell items for more by not posting prices up front. They want to be able to up-sell their customers to ever higher dollar amounts. Again, they're at a festival, not a Jaguar dealership or haute couture dress shop. Besides, selling the same items at different prices, depending on how hard customers can be sold, is just plain dishonest.

There's a fellow I know in Carson City, Nevada, who runs a disc jockey service. When a prospective client calls to ask for his rates, he never quotes prices up front. Instead, he immediately goes into sell mode. He asks the prospect where their event is going to be held, who the caterer will be, and how formal is the dress level. The more he knows about how much the prospect is already planning to spend, the higher his rate goes. I find that method of setting prices dishonest and offensive.

If a customer wants something extra, it's reasonable to charge extra for it. But it is not reasonable to charge some customers more than others for identical items, just because some can be hard-sold into paying more.

Festival vendors, in particular, are shooting themselves in the feet if they do not openly display pricing on all their items. I've encountered pushy merchants who insist they can get more money out of customers by sell-sell-selling them on their items. Meanwhile, how many potential buyers are walking by without stopping, because they don't want to have to ask how much an item costs? Even if a pushy vendor can wrench more money out of some customers, is that worth the missed sales of people who hate a hardcore pitchman?

You may wonder why I am stressing posting prices on merchandise. Perhaps it never occurred to you NOT to post prices. That means you likely think, as I do, that pricing your items is a no-brainer; of course merchandise should be displayed with clearly marked prices. Others I have met, however, have their minds dead set against displaying prices. Those vendors love the hard sell. They think hard selling is fun, and they feel strongly they make more money. If that describes you, here's what I suggest: Try it both ways. Print up nice looking price tags for some events. Do some other events without displaying prices. See which method results in more money for your effort.

You'll Need A Vehicle

I'm sure you have thought of this. You can't carry a tent, display tables and shelves, equipment, and all your stock to an event in an economy car. However, if you're smarter than I was, you won't buy a big vehicle before you know for sure how you'll be using it!

By the time you finish this book, you may become tired of reading my warnings that you should start small and build up as you go. If I had followed this advice when I started, I could have saved myself several thousand dollars of precious misspent funds, and I'd have saved myself a lot of redundant work and wasted time. OMG, all the time, hard work, and money I wasted. It's depressing to think about it.

RENT a truck for your first few events. Yes, it's more trouble to go to Ryder or U-Haul to pick up a vehicle, drive it back to the house, load it, then drive it to an event and unload it. What seems extra trouble will save you huge expense and wasted time.

I got it in my head I needed a big travel/hauling vehicle right from the get-go, so I bought an old, used motorhome on eBay. It was my first and only really bad experience using the online auction site. The seller completely ripped me off. The motorhome was located in Panama City, Florida – a long trip from Reno, Nevada. I made the mistake of not picking up the vehicle right away, so it was too late for me to file a complaint with eBay to demand a refund.

I'm not a complete fool. I sent the seller many questions about the vehicle, explaining how I intended to use the motorhome, and that I would be driving it cross country immediately after picking it up. He assured me the motorhome was road-worthy, ready to travel.

It was very much not road-worthy, not ready to be driven anywhere.

My gal and I decided to make a fun trip of picking up the vehicle, which required advance planning. That's why we were delayed making the trip. We flew to Panama City almost two months after the auction closed. I had to send payment within five days after auction closed, so the dishonest seller already had my money. And he'd already spent it.When we arrived, we discovered the motorhome had been sitting on a dirt lot for quite some time. This was in Florida, so moisture had taken its toll on the vehicle, inside and out. For a vehicle with only 68,000 miles on its odometer, it looked awful. The brakes were shot, transmission slipped, gas tank leaked. It was unbelievable the scumbag seller had so misrepresented the condition of this beat up motorhome in his listing.

I drove it – very carefully, due to almost non-existent brakes – to a nearby truck repair center. I was prepared to junk the thing and take my loss, lesson learned. A nice mechanic at the truck repair shop looked it over. He determined the chassis and frame were still sound, tires and suspension looked good. The vehicle could be repaired and returned to useful condition, but the work would cost almost two grand and take about a week.

First vehicle I purchased for my vending business, affectionately nick-named "The Beast."

My gal and I were in a rented car, and, as I said, we had already planned to make an adventure of this trip. I called the car rental service, extended the rental for a week, and we took off for a road trip up the coast while the motorhome went into the shop for extensive repairs. Our trip cost way more than expected, but we tried not to dwell on our misfortune.

After our trip up the coast, my gal flew home to Reno from New York, and I drove the rental car back to Panama City. The truck repair center did a remarkable job. That old motorhome, which we had nick-named "The Beast" by then, made the 2,500 mile drive from Panama City to Reno without incident. What an adventure!

I used The Beast for my first few events, but it was apparent almost immediately that it was not the right vehicle for my purposes. A year after the wild – and costly – adventure of buying it, I posted an ad on Craigslist and sold The Beast for less than half what I had paid for it.

Wiser from that experience, I returned to eBay to search for a deal on a vehicle to use for my vending business. This time I found a shuttle van being sold by a fellow in Denver, Colorado. It was an oversized van that most consumers had no use for, so the sale price was quite low for such a large vehicle.

My bid won the auction, and I scheduled a flight to Denver for just five days later. Booking a flight with such short notice costs more than scheduling a flight weeks in advance, as you likely know, but I had learned my lesson from my previous vehicle buying experience on eBay. By picking up the vehicle within a week of the auction ending,

I did not have to send payment ahead of time. If the shuttle van had not been as the seller described, I would have backed out of the purchase and only been out the cost of flights to and from Denver.

Fortunately, this time I was dealing with an honest seller. He was a nice younger fellow who had used the van to transport his motorcycles to and from motocross competitions. In spite of being used to haul motorcycles, the shuttle van was remarkably clean and ran perfectly. It drove nicely back to Reno.

Now I had a powerful, big van. It was perfect for carrying and storing back-up stock of cups and other dry products that take up a surprising amount of space. For example, I found a deal on coffee stir straws on Craigslist from a diner that was going out of business. It was a case of fifty boxes containing a thousand stir straws per box. It was a heck of a bargain, but fifty thousand stir straws take up a lot of room. The shuttle van provided the space to carry and store that huge case of stir straws. I did not need to buy stir straws again for over a decade.

I was also acquiring more and more equipment for my set-up. Back to eBay to find a trailer for hauling my mobile shop. A good deal came up on a "toy hauler" trailer in Phoenix. Again, I did not wait to go pick up my purchase. Three days after the auction closed, I drove my big shuttle van to Arizona and paid for the trailer *after* having a chance to check it out.

That shuttle van and toy hauler became my Tropic Hut rig for many years.

My "rig" served me well, and I have many fond memories of driving it to festivals all over the Southwest. However, if I had been smarter about managing my funds, I would not have invested in such big vehicles so early. Most cities and Home Owner Associations have strict rules about parking oversized vehicles in suburban neighborhoods. I didn't have a house in the country with a huge lot where I could park my rig. That meant finding an RV storage facility. If I ever have the funds, RV storage is the next business to go into.

**My Tropic Hut mobile rig –
Bought both the shuttle van and
"toy hauler" trailer on eBay!**

RV storage facilities are astonishingly expensive. And even at sky high prices, it was difficult to find a facility nearby with spaces available. Some storage lots would charge eighty dollars <u>each</u> for the two spaces my rig required. These were dirt lots in remote areas of town. No covered parking, no electrical hook-ups, no dump station, no lighting; just a fence around an empty lot. After extensive searching, I found a place that made a deal to store both my vehicles for a hundred dollars per month.

That's a hundred bucks per month year round – $1,200 for twelve months for storage alone. Considering the price of the vehicles, the cost of fuel and maintenance, insurance, registration, and so on, I would have been much better off to rent a truck for each event for the first couple years.

Over and over I repeat this advice; don't try to go too big too fast. It's so tempting, I know. If you have the funds, you want to jump in all the way, right from the start. It doesn't matter if you can afford it, starting too big too fast means you will assuredly make mistakes. Later on, you will be grateful to have stayed nimble early on. Staying small at first allows a vendor to make adjustments quickly and inexpensively.

This is yet another advantage to a mobile vending business over a fixed position shop. Starting up a restaurant or retail store means you have to invest in many things before knowing if they will work or not. You may become eager, as I did, and buy more than you should when starting up a mobile shop. But a few hundred or a few thousand dollars spent to start a vending business pales compared to the many thousands spent to start a retail store before opening for day one of business.

Meet Sherrie, Famous Dave's Sauce Girl at Reno Wings Cook-Off. My stand sent them cold drinks, and they fed us wings. Meeting and bartering with other vendors is part of the fun of doing festivals.

Jarvis Hooten

8 Okay, Let's Do Some Events!

Setting Up – Welcome To Chaos

The vendor set-up stage of an event can be a nightmare or a breeze, and that depends almost entirely on the organizer. At some events, you will arrive to find the organizer has an entire staff of professional people with radios and clip boards, all wearing matching shirts so they can be easily identified. Each vendor's space assignment is clearly marked, electrical power supplies are set up and ready for use.

At other events you will discover the term "organizer" is not the right word to describe the person in charge. It may take twenty minutes just to find the organizer in the first place. Vendor spaces are being assigned as the vendors arrive. When you finally find the (dis)organizer, it goes something like this:

"Hi, I'm here with Tropic Hut."

"Yeah, hi," says the organizer. "Um, what do you sell?" I briefly describe my products, all of which were defined in detail on my contract, of course.

"Okay, how about we put you over there by the picnic tables?" At least he's had the foresight to put a food vendor by picnic tables. But when I get to the location, I notice I'll be right next to another beverage vendor. That's not the end of the world, as some vendors think, but it's not ideal, either.

I go looking for the organizer again. This time it only takes fifteen minutes to find him. "Is it possible to locate me a little further up the row, so I'm not right next to another drink vendor?"

"Yeah, sure. Just move up the row a bit and pick the spot you like. Should be fine."

"While I have you," I begin to ask, tentatively, "where do I find power?"

"Oh, you need power?" comes the response I was afraid of. The contract for this event clearly states every vendor will receive a 20 Amp circuit of electrical power, and I paid fifty dollars extra to have a second 20 Amp circuit.

"Yes, I need power," and thus begins a nightmare set-up.

Note to vendors who will need electrical power: This is a surprisingly common problem. Many events forbid generators, understandably, because generators make a lot of noise and belch out smelly fumes. But these same events often do not provide the electrical power many vendors rely on. This isn't the 18th Century. Blenders and coffee brewers have to have electrical power. So do soldering tools used by crafters and blowers used by inflatables. You'd think event organizers would understand that. I've been to events where the dunderhead organizer didn't even think to have electrical outlets at the bandstand. The first band was scheduled to start in a few hours, and they were stretching extension cords to the stage from nearby houses. It doesn't hurt to remind organizers several times beforehand that you cannot operate without electrical power.

Even the best organized events can be stressful during the set-up stage. Poorly organized events will test the patience of a saint. Try to keep your wits. It may seem as if you are in a war zone, but remember, it's just a festival.

To minimize the stress, do all you can to make sure your own act is together. Figure out ahead of time how you are going to set up your stand, where equipment will be placed, where you will store your back-up stock, and how you will run cords to your electrical devices. If you just bought a new tent, take it out of the box and learn how to set it up before you go to an event.

There's a reason why the invention of the wheel was important to humans. It makes moving loads much faster and easier. Yes, really – wheels are amazing! Get your stuff on wheels, and not little dainty wheeled carts for moving small shelves around the house. Those small hand carts with little caster wheels are practically useless to us vendors.

You need big wheels, preferably pneumatic (air filled) tires to roll your stuff around on. Sometimes you will be rolling your equipment and boxes across nice, smooth concrete sidewalks. Other times you will need to go across a hundred feet of gravel, dirt and grass between your vehicle and your stand.

I have installed large, expensive casters on all my equipment, and I bought the best, priciest hand cart available. The hand cart alone cost almost $300, but it has paid for itself many times over by how much easier it makes moving loads across rough terrain.

Here's a helpful tip if you get a cart with pneumatic tires, which I highly recommend. (And, by the way, why can't they just call them "air filled" tires?) Be sure to carry a bicycle pump. For some reason, the pneumatic tires on carts and dollies don't hold air pressure well. Nice, firm, air-filled tires are dreamy for rolling heavy loads on dollies or carts. That dreamy advantage is lost if the tires are flat.

Your objective is to get your vehicle unloaded and off the festival grounds as quickly as possible. Once you have all your gear in your space and your vehicle is out of the way, you can relax and take your time to organize the small stuff.

Here's one more tip for loading and unloading to save you from a painful experience. This may seem a strange thing to suggest, but you want to keep your mouth closed and your teeth together. You'll be surprised how often you bump your chin while moving large objects. If your mouth is open when you bump your chin, it will cause your teeth to slam together. And if your tongue is between your teeth when that happens, you can get a serious ouch.

At one event I was rolling a freezer on my dolly across a long stretch of grass. The grass was firm and my dolly has nice big tires, so I was able to roll along at a pretty fast clip. I did not see the brick in the grass. When the dolly tire hit that brick, it came to an abrupt, complete stop. I, on the other hand, did not stop so quickly. My chin slammed into the top of the freezer, and I bit down on my tongue so hard it almost made me black out from the pain. It was all I could do to set the freezer upright before I sat down heavily in the grass with stars flashing before my eyes. From that day on I've made a conscious commitment to keep my mouth closed while loading and unloading.

Making Sales – What This Is All About

I'll never forget my first sale at my first event. After several stressful hours of loading in, setting up, having my first health department inspection, finding a place to get ice, figuring out how to get electrical power to all my devices, and all the other trauma that goes with assembling a vending stand, I was finally ready for business.

Visitors had started milling around the event before I had finished setting up. Some of them stopped and looked at my menu but moved on. I greeted folks with a pleasant "Hey there!" not really knowing what to say.

After a while a woman stepped up to my stand and looked over my menu in earnest. She turned to me and asked for a nachos platter and began to reach into her purse. Wow, here was a complete stranger, someone I had never seen before in my life, who wanted to buy something I had made.

"Coming right up!" I responded cheerfully. Then I fumbled around to remember how I had planned to serve a nachos platter. Oh yeah, I would put chips into the large compartment of a food tray, then ladle my home-made cheese sauce into the small compartments. This way, I figured, unlike nachos from most other vendors, the chips would stay separate from the cheese sauce and thus stay crisp.

I handed the lady her nachos platter and collected payment. She started to walk away and I just couldn't help myself. I said, "Wait, I have to know how you like my queso recipe!"

She smiled and said, "Oh, sure," and opened the food container, dipped a chip in the queso sauce and took a bite. "Hey, that's really good!"

I was hooked. After all the work, the planning, the preparation, this was the pay-off. Being a vendor, I thought to myself, is going to be fun.

Several years of vending later, that pay-off – having people buy and enjoy my products – is still really fun. I've also learned a few tricks about the actual selling process.

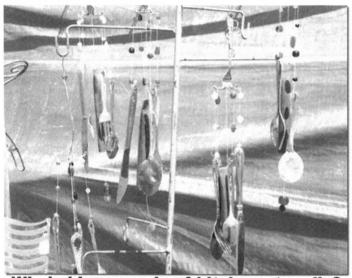

Wind chimes made of kitchen utencils? Gotta love creative craft vendors!

How Much To Charge

Setting your prices is sometimes a delicate art. Earlier I made the argument that it's dishonest to charge different prices for identical items, depending on how hard a customer can be sold. This is true at any one given event, but from one event to another, price adjustments are completely acceptable and even necessary.

Competition will be your best determiner of pricing. This is the magnificence of free enterprise. If another vendor is selling items similar to yours at exorbitant prices, how easy it is to under-cut them. On the other hand, sometimes you'll find yourself at events where other vendors are selling way too cheap. This is why I always bring multiple menu sheets to events.

Doh! Such a beautiful – and probably expensive – custom skin on this exotic meats trailer, but they misspelled TWO of their own products. Otherwise, this would be really great signage.

You do go to festivals, don't you? I mean, surely you are not considering being a festival vendor if you don't like going to festivals, right? Now is the time – before you work your first event – to attend a few festivals with research in mind. You're no longer simply a festival-goer; you're a festival vendor. Observe other vendors, see what appeals to you and what seems to work. Take lots of pictures. And check out the prices other vendors are charging.

At one festival I worked, the organizer had allowed in a Lion's Club booth, which was fundraising by selling coffee for a dollar a cup. My usual price was three dollars a cup. To be fair, it should be pointed out the Lion's Club folks were selling low quality, weak coffee in tiny ten ounce cups. My stand sells premium coffee in sixteen ounce cups. Nonetheless, I dropped my price on the spot to two dollars and did quite well competing against the cheaper vendor. Fortunately, it was a well attended event with plenty of coffee customers to go around. I'm all for a good civic organization raising funds, but the event organizer should not have pitted me against a charity vendor selling the same product.

Another important strategy for setting prices is to offer a range to choose from. Most festival-goers have dollar amounts in their minds of what they are prepared to spend. Some people will buy a similar item to what you are selling from another vendor at a higher price, simply because the other price fits what they expect to pay for such an item. Some customers have lower price expectations. Also, a higher price gives the illusion of higher quality to some buyers. Others don't fall for the high-price-equals-high-quality illusion. To reach customers from the high end to the low end of price expectations, offer a range of price points in your products. Have low, medium, and high priced items within your scope of product types.

All your price points should equate value to the customer. That is, your low priced items should not seem cheap and low quality, and high priced items should not seem exaggerated or overdone, just to increase their price. Every buyer should feel they are getting good value for the price.

Your prices should have a low-to-high range, but that range needs to be within reasonable expectations. The same vendor should not offer items ranging from under two dollars to over two thousand dollars. We should all stay in our lanes.

As you have probably gathered, I am a big believer in banners and a further big believer in using photos in my signage. That's because I have seen first hand how effective these advertising tools are to mobile vendors. Signage is the only advertising medium a mobile vendor uses. Can you see any benefit for a vendor to buy radio, TV, or Internet ads? Event organizers use media advertising to draw crowds to events. On the event grounds, it's our signs that draw crowds to our booths.

Putting pictures of my products in my signs just made sense to me. Fast food restaurants use pictures of their products in their signs. Does anyone not know what a Big Mac looks like? Or two

Jack-In-The-Box Tacos? Or a Denny's omelet? I'll bet you can picture those items in your head right now. But go to any of those restaurants and you'll find pictures of those items in their signs and menus. Pictures sell, even if the buyer doesn't need a picture to know what the item looks like. Pictures sell all the more for us vendors, because the buyer may not know what the item looks like. A picture shows them what they are getting *and* makes that item look more enticing.

Come to find out, my belief in pictures is not just a simple idea that made sense to me; it is a highly researched principle in marketing. At the Nevada State Fair a few years ago, a young man was walking by my booth and stopped suddenly when he saw my banners. He began to smile more and more as he looked over all my signage. Finally he stepped up and told me he had just graduated from UNR (University of Nevada Reno) with a marketing degree. He had spent an entire course studying the effectiveness of pictures in advertising, and he was delighted and amazed to see so many pictures in my banners.

This was very flattering, of course, but it confirmed what I already knew instinctively. Good signage *with pictures* is good marketing. Your signs are your salesmen. Get good ones and put them to work for you.

The appearance of your stand itself is another strong factor in attracting customers. It needs to look clean and orderly, of course, but it helps if it also looks *cool*.

Giving your stand a theme makes it easy to figure out how to decorate it. If you're selling ice cream, perhaps your stand could have an old fashioned theme. Find replicas of old diner signs or Route 66 road signs and hang them around your booth. A booth selling cell phone accessories could go the opposite direction with a futuristic theme. Use clear acrylic display boxes on stark white or silver surfaces. If you sell jewelry you could create an air of regal elegance with purple velvet on the tables and sidewalls of your booth. A sunglasses booth could have beach balls on the counters and a surf board leaning against a corner to create a fun-in-the-sun atmosphere.

The crowning touch to the appearance of your stand is to decorate the very people working it. You and your staff, even if it's only two of you, should wear something uniform. Just wearing matching hats or aprons will make your entire stand seem far more professional. When you've been in business a while and have decided on your theme and products, get matching shirts that fit your booth's image to finish the look.

Go to a few events as a visitor. Try to put your own product likes and dislikes out of your mind. That is, if you love fantasy figurines or your favorite carnival snack is corn dogs, try not to seek out those stands. Allow your eyes to be drawn to any kind of vendor that stands out, regardless what they are selling. What made that vendor catch your attention? Could you use those same techniques in your own stand?

Bargaining

Everyone loves a deal, and an unexpected deal is even better. I'm surprised that some vendors will not bargain with customers. If a guy and gal stop in front of your stand to look over your items, but you can see they are hesitating, make an offer they don't expect. A smart vendor would say, "Tell you what, those are usually six dollars each, but you two look so good together, I'll sell you two for ten bucks."

Making a little less on a sale is better than not making a sale at all. And it's very satisfying to let customers feel they got more than they expected. Most people who attend festivals have a loose figure in mind for the amount of money they expect to spend. Every dollar they spend at another vendor is a dollar less they will spend at your booth.

You may think this goes against my earlier comments about hard-selling, but this is bargaining, not selling. Your prices are clearly marked. The customer fully understands you are offering an unadvertised deal. Many customers regard bargaining as part of the fun of dealing with festival vendors. A cashier at Arby's or Target can't make an on-the-spot deal.

Bargaining is for slow times at a festival. When a crowd of eager buyers is lined up in front of your stand, everyone pays flat price. Bargaining during busy stretches is unnecessary. It slows down service time, and it makes folks at the back of the line feel gypped if they are not offered similar deals to what others were offered.

Have Fun With Your Customers

Finally, to attract customers, festival vendors must be willing to engage with people. This is not a business for wallflowers. Even if a vendor just smiles and greets people as they walk by, that attracts far more customers than vendors who hide in their stands, not acknowledging anyone.

Jarvis Hooten

Come up with clever ways to start conversations. When you see someone wearing a Green Bay football jersey, say, "Packers fans love our pulled pork sandwiches!" A home decor merchandise vendor at an event in June might say, "Our candle holders make terrific Fourth-Of-July gifts!" If a person in brightly colored shoes walks by, say, "Our products are custom designed to go with neon sneakers."

Festivals are supposed to be fun. That's why people go to them. Vendors who have fun with attendees are guaranteed to turn passers-by into customers.

The Importance Of
Maximizing Rushes

People tend to move around events in waves. It is rare for a vendor to have steady, consistent business all day long. Food vendors in particular have rushes and lulls. At some events the reason for this is obvious. At a music festival, people get up and visit vendors in between bands. At a sporting event, people go to the vendors between heats or during half time.

The most dramatic vendor rushes I've experienced are at hot air ballooning events. The opening attraction each morning of a ballooning event is the dawn patrol. Before sunrise, one or two balloons equipped with lights and sensing devices go aloft to check conditions. This requires special licensing for the pilots of those balloons. The dawn patrol has become a major attraction because, in the pitch darkness, the one or two balloons firing their gas flames make spectacular displays of light and color against the black sky. It's astonishing to see thousands of people arriving at an event at 4:00 AM.

After the dawn patrol, the crowd has about a two hour wait for the next big attraction, which is the mass lift off of balloons after sunrise. During the lull is when the crowds head for the booths. In a matter of minutes, vendors who had been doing no business at all suddenly have long lines in front of their stands. It's really intense.

Here's the important lesson to be learned: Vendors succeed by their ability to maximize rushes. If a rush lasts thirty minutes, and it takes you three minutes to fill each order, that's ten customers you'd serve. If you can fill each order in one minute, you'd serve thirty customers during the same rush.

Whatever your product is, figure out the best way to make your order-to-delivery time as fast as possible during a rush. Experiment with your booth layout, rearrange the placement of bins and holding appliances, try to eliminate redundant steps, make the flow of your operation efficient, smooth, and, most of all, *fast*.

This was the secret to the success of the original McDonald's restaurant. The McDonald broth-

ers took their staff to a tennis court and drew out-
lines of the kitchen layout on the court surface.
The staff acted out a busy lunch rush over and over
with different arrangements of the layout. This
was how the original McDonald's famously per-
fected fast food service.

**Don't forget lights for your stand.
This is my Tropic Hut booth at
Albuquergue International Balloon
Fiesta. It's 4:30 AM.**

Simple advance preparation can help you
take maximum advantage of rushes. For example,

have plenty of small bills available to make change. I started out thinking one hundred bucks worth of small bills – fifty in ones and fifty in fives – was enough for my cash register. Now I begin each event with a hundred in ones and two hundred in fives ($300 total). This way I'm prepared when twenty customers in a row pay for their purchases with twenty dollar bills. I also learned to round off the prices of my items to even dollars. Coins are way too much hassle.

Keep your back-up stock organized and easily reachable. You don't want to have to move multiple boxes and dig around for several minutes if you run out of cups during a rush.

Learn to pace your prep with multiple items. Let's say your most popular item is a turkey and bacon wrap. Making each wrap requires reaching into the bread holder for a wrap, reaching into the refrigerator for the turkey, then the bacon, lettuce, cheese and sauce. A line forms in front of your stand, and someone orders the turkey and bacon wrap. Now is the time to reach in the bread holder and take out <u>four</u> wraps, reach in the refrigerator and take out four portions of turkey, bacon, and so on. You're making the one wrap that just sold, but you're ready for the next three that are almost certain to sell in the next few minutes. With a growing line in front of your stand, you'll easily use those items right away.

I witnessed both good and bad rush-handling stands at Albuquerque International Balloon Fiesta a few years ago. As I described earlier, hot air balloon events have the most intense rushes of any kind of festival I've seen. A couple ladies were selling taco salads a few stands down the row from mine. The taco salads were terrific, but each one took six to eight minutes to prepare. The ladies had not figured out ways to expedite their prep time. Every day lines formed in front of all the food stands during the rush, but the taco salad ladies' line moved terribly slowly. Those hard working ladies could have doubled or tripled their sales simply by finding ways to fill orders faster.

Further down the row from the taco salad ladies was a breakfast burrito stand. To be fair, I must include the fact that the breakfast burrito stand was larger and had more employees than the two ladies with the taco salad stand, but that's the point. The breakfast burrito stand was better prepared. When a line formed in front of the breakfast burrito stand, each customer got their order filled within a minute.

That turnaround time of one minute or less became my goal, and I have made it happen. Some orders take slightly longer and others shorter, but on average my stand fills all orders in less than sixty seconds. During rushes, I've worked with my staff to go into "overdrive" mode, when we trim our order fill time down to just over thirty seconds.

Of course, not all stands can trim their order fill time down to under sixty seconds. I sell mostly beverages, which are easier and faster to serve than food items, so my stand has an advantage. Still, if your average order fill time is over three minutes, especially during a rush, it's time to examine how you are preparing and serving your items and consider changing or eliminating items that are time hogs. The focus is on your *average* turnaround time for filling orders. If you have a chicken wings stand, and one of your menu options is a family pack that comes with sides and beverages, it's understandable that you can't fill that order in under a minute.

Now that I've been in the business a while, the first thing I think when I see an impressive stand like this is how much trouble it must be to set up!

One of the best techniques for expediting order filling is to have separate "Order Here" and "Pick Up Here" counters or windows. One person

Jarvis Hooten

of your staff works the register taking orders while the rest of the staff fills the orders. This not only keeps your line moving, it keeps only one person handling the money. That means your most trusted, best customer service person works the register. It also means the person handling cash is not handling food.

Albuquerque International Balloon Fiesta taught me the importance of speed during rushes. That event also taught me the foolishness of taking on too much too soon with a new vending business. Although I had done several events by then, I was still in my first year and still establishing my product line. Balloon Fiesta is attended by more than three quarters of a million people over a nine day period. It was way bigger than I was ready to handle. I made less than half the money I could have made at that event, had I been better prepared and more experienced.

My very supportive girlfriend came with me to help at Balloon Fiesta. One of our favorite funny stories happened during an early morning at the balloon field.

We got to the festival grounds at 3:30 AM to start brewing coffee and prepping food items. The area was eerily quiet with only us vendors and event staff making any sounds at all. Then, at 5:00 AM, here came the insane crush of people. My gal worked the cash register and I filled orders as fast as our hands and feet could move.

After about an hour of this intense pace, I felt a tug on my shirt sleeve. I was turned away from the front of the stand, starting up another giant urn of coffee to brew. When I turned around, I looked into the pale, exhausted face of my gal. Too little sleep and too much stress had got the best of her. She was holding a $100 bill. "Your gonna have to make change for this customer," she muttered. "I'm way too tired to figure it out."

We've laughed many times about that fateful morning in New Mexico. But we learned our lesson. It was two years before I even tried to book my stand into a massive event like that.

Resolving Customer Conflicts

Eventually, no matter how wondrous and delightful your products are, you're going to encounter an unsatisfied customer. If their complaint is legitimate, you want to make it right immediately, of course. Perhaps they discovered a scratch in the face of a watch you sold them. Maybe their funnel cake was over-cooked and greasy. These are legitimate complaints, and these customers should get refunds or replacement products right away. To make these customers really happy, throw in a bonus item as your way of making up for the flawed product.

You will also encounter unsatisfied customers whose complaints are not legitimate. You sell a perfect product to this kind of customer, and they come back and say they don't like it. Give these customers their money back even faster than the customers with legitimate complaints. Get them away from your stand and out of your life as quickly as possible. Some people go through life being pains in the rear to merchants. Such people are not worth arguing with.

At the Nevada State Fair a few years ago a very attractive girl approached my stand. She was wearing tight designer jeans, high heals, a lacy blouse, and lots of jewelry. This was how she dressed to go to the state fair. Oh, she was a looker, to be sure, but it was obvious she knew she was a looker and expected to be treated as royalty.

She asked about my blended coffee drinks. Did I have soy milk? No, but I did have nonfat milk. Okay, she'd take a blended coffee drink with nonfat milk. Then she proceeded to tell me exactly how to prepare it.

"I want just a little brown sugar but put in extra mocha syrup. Be sure you blend it long enough so there are no chunks of ice. Oh, and I want it with half regular coffee and half decaf."

"Yes, your highness," I thought to myself, like I don't know how to make one of the most popular drinks on my menu. I made the drink to her specifications and presented it to her. She started to walk away, took a sip of the drink, then walked back.

"This isn't what I wanted. Can I have a refund?"

I had already taken her money back out of the register. "No problem. Here you go. Enjoy the fair!" I said.

Some vendors allow themselves to get upset at this kind of customer and will actually argue with them. I could have told the princess, "Hey, that's one of the most popular drinks on my menu, and I specially made it exactly the way you ordered it. What do you mean it's not what you wanted?" I might have been completely justified to feel that way, but it is absolutely not the way to deal with a problem customer.

Some people go through life being pains in the neck. That's just the way they are. Arguing with them, pointing out the unfairness of their demands, or trying to reason with them is counterproductive. It wastes your time and energy. That's reason enough not to argue with a problem customer, but also remember that other customers may be watching. If they see you being the bigger person when dealing with a problem customer, their impression of you will go up.

To be clear, I am not suggesting you take the position that "the customer is always right," because the customer is not always right. If someone ever came back to my stand with an empty cup and said, "That drink wasn't what I wanted. Could I get my money back?" I would not give them a full refund. They finished the entire drink and then wanted a refund? This has never happened, but the way I would probably handle it would be to give them a half refund of their purchase. The customer is absolutely wrong to demand a refund *after* consuming a product, but I will be the bigger person and not argue with them.

I once listened to an audio presentation by Richard C. Huseman, co-author of "Managing The Equity Factor Or 'After All I've Done For You.'" The Equity Factor is a brilliant concept that has stuck with me ever since listening to that cassette tape.

All of us have built-in senses of balance in our relationships, both personal and business. Our focus here is on business, of course. For most people, this sense of balance between give and take is fairly even. Most employees give a fair day's work for a fair day's pay. Likewise, most employers pay a fair day's wage for a fair day's work. If this equity factor is out of balance, eventually one of the parties will take action to correct it. Employees who feel underpaid and under-appreciated will seek other jobs. Employers who feel they aren't getting adequate performances from employees will fire them.

The same applies in retail. We vendors offer good products at fair prices, and customers want to feel they are receiving good value for their money.

For some people, however, the sense of balance, their "Equity Factor," is skewed. Some people are Benefactors; always giving or doing more than they need to. These people rarely complain to a merchant or ask for their money back.

Then there are the Entitles; people who think they deserve more than they give. Our country is developing a shamefully high percentage of Entitles, and too many politicians woo these selfish people's votes by giving the productivity of a few to the entitlements of many, but that's for another discussion.

As vendors, we are wise to lean toward being benefactors with customers. Don't give away the store trying to please everyone, but try to make most customers leave your shop feeling they got more than they expected. When you do encounter an Entitled, be the bigger person and send them on their way, away from your stand, as quickly as possible. Don't allow yourself to be taken advantage of, but also don't expend too much energy on a lout. Life is too short to waste time on selfish scumbags. There are plenty of good folks to make up for the bad experiences.

Will That Be Cash Or Credit?

In our wireless digital age of smart phones, accepting credit and debit cards has become remarkably easy for vendors. Merchandise vendors in particular should definitely find a way to accept plastic payment.

If you sell high ticket items, you're certain to make a lot of credit card sales. I started my concessions business in 2005, before there were smart phones. I spent a bunch of money on a merchant account with a portable card reader and printer. The device worked through a cell service connection – not the service for my cell phone; the device required its own cellular account. The fixed monthly fees were almost a hundred dollars, whether I made a single sale or not. But it was the coolest mobile option available at the time.

Now we vendors have far better ways of accepting credit cards using our smart phones. You can attach a tiny card reading device to your iPhone or other smart phone and accept credit cards with no monthly service fees of any kind. The transaction fee percentage might be a bit higher than if you had a full merchant credit card account, but that added cost per transaction is outweighed by not having monthly service fees.

My favorite of these cell phone credit card services is called The Square (https://squareup.com/). This service provides a free card reader that's about the size of a postage stamp. It plugs into your smart phone's audio jack. The Square can also be used with a digital tablet, allowing a vendor to create an entire menu with elaborate pictures and use the tablet as a cash register. The Square was so successful that PayPal now offers a similar card-swipe device.

The only drawback to The Square and similar devices is the customer does not physically sign for their purchase, and they receive no printed receipt.

Instead, they "cyber sign" by using a finger on your iPhone's or iPad's touch screen. If they desire a receipt, they give you their e-mail address or text number, and a digital receipt is sent to them. This may pose a problem for large ticket items or for customers who insist on a paper receipt for every purchase. But in today's technically hip society, most people, especially young folks, are completely comfortable with digital signatures and no receipts for small purchases.

A regular merchant account is only beneficial for businesses that do thousands of dollars in credit sales per week year round. Merchant accounts involve lengthy applications with banks, credit checks, and set-up fees. The processing fee is only a few tenths of a percent less expensive on a merchant account. That's hardly worth the trouble for us mobile vendors.

A mobile credit card account is much easier to set up, and it's completely free to maintain. Only time a fee is charged is when a transaction is processed. However, there are still important restrictions to be aware of. If you start a credit card account with Square or Paypal, and you register your business as a t-shirt shop, they may put a hold on a transaction for two thousand dollars.

Banks and creditors have to follow strict government regulations. One of those regulations is making sure only legal transactions are being processed through their systems. PayPal is notorious for freezing or even closing accounts on businesses that start selling things other than what they registered to sell. Those sales may be perfectly legitimate. Maybe a t-shirt vendor had some furniture to sell. Nonetheless, a two thousand dollar purchase looks suspicious on an account that usually does transactions under twenty dollars. If you change products or services, let your credit card processing company know abut it.

After The Event – Keeping Records

You're exhausted. Your feet hurt. Loading out took longer than expected, and you scraped your knuckles while carrying a heavy box. All you want to do is get back home or to the hotel room, take a shower, and sit by the air conditioner. Go ahead and relax, get comfortable and apply aloe gel to your sunburned skin, but do not allow several days to go by before you count your cash and write down how much business you did.

Some of my friends have advised me not to touch the subject I'm about to bring up. They think I might be recommending dishonest behavior or inviting trouble from the terrifying IRS. But it's something every vendor will think of on their own, so I want to address it.

Since vending is a mostly cash business it's entirely possible a couple hundred dollars of your sales might *somehow* not get included in your written record for each event. Yes, there are tax advantages to a cash business. Just keep in mind the IRS is aware of this. Don't go crazy and only report a fifth of your cash sales. (For the purposes of this book, I want to state clearly and emphatically that my business accounts for and reports every dollar of sales without exception and without fail.)

Nice looking merchandise stand – well organized with attractive displays. But what are they selling? Books? Artistic photo prints? CDs? Hard to tell from a distance. Some handsome banners across the top are all this stand needs.

The IRS audited me in 2002 for a previous business I owned. The experience literally changed my life and tarnished my perspective of this great country we live in. The IRS is the closest thing we Americans have to a despotic ruler. Our US tax code is downright dishonest and, in some cases, just plain cruel. After being audited I became a strong proponent of Fair Tax (http://www.fair-tax.org/). It will be years before enough support for Fair Tax builds up and the program is implemented, so, for now, get used to the horrible IRS system and try to make the best of it.

If you have never reported income from a business on your Income Tax return before, it's a good idea to get a Schedule C form ahead of time, so you can see how the IRS expects you to report your revenue and expenses. Go to http://www.irs.gov/, click "Forms And Publications" then click "1040 Sch C." The IRS looks at business expenses differently from the real world. It helps to learn their absurdities before you start record keeping. This will make sorting receipts easier.

Almost all businesses are not profitable in their first years. The IRS does not want to hear this from a small business start-up. They want you to amortize your big first year equipment expenses, so that your business appears to have made a profit in its very first year.

My first year in the vending business was not at all profitable, not by reasonable people's standards. I pulled money out of savings and took out a loan, so my overall financial status showed me to be much poorer at the end of that year than at the beginning of the year. Any sensible person would say I had not made any money; I had lost money.

It was money spent building a business in hopes of future gains, so perhaps it could be considered not to have been "lost," but it was funds gone out of my revenue for that year, so it certainly wasn't income.

However, by that time I had run a previous business and had experienced my IRS audit. I knew what they were looking for. My Schedule C for that year was complete fiction. I'm not kidding. I just made up numbers out of thin air, not even adding up my receipts or looking at my sales records. If I had reported my actual expenses – if I had been totally honest and followed IRS code perfectly – I would have shown a loss for the year. Showing no income, even in the first year of a small business start-up, is a red flag to invite an audit from the IRS. And an audit is how the IRS finds some way to force citizens to pay taxes they don't really owe, in my experience. I wanted my business to show some small profit so I could have something to pay taxes on.

That's right. I "cooked my books" in order to *pay more taxes*, not to evade them. This is how bad our tax code is. You may have completely legitimate business expenses. You may report every dollar of income, even the fifty bucks your cousin gave you to help him paint his deck. That's not enough for the IRS. If they think they can get more money out of you, they will find a way, no matter how dishonest or absurd, to make you pay more taxes. Maybe IRS agents were all bullied as kids. Maybe their moms didn't hug them enough. Whatever the reason, my experience with IRS agents is they enjoy sticking it to us taxpayers. I have learned to fix the numbers in my Schedule C to what the IRS wants to see, not what they really are.

Run-A-Muccca Motorcycle Festival – Motocross jumpers are popular at many biker events. I got to watch their shows right from my stand.

The areas small businesses get into trouble are travel expense, vehicle expense, and home office expense. Vehicle expense is where they got me. I used to be in the entertainment biz. I owned and hosted a traveling game show. How's that for a wacky way to make a living? An agency booked my show, and in a six year period I performed at colleges and shopping malls in forty-three states. It was a very fun and memorable time of my life.

To my utter shock and dismay, when the IRS audited me it was because they had decided to disallow *ALL* my travel and vehicle expense. In their view, since I traveled to do a show and then traveled on to do the next show and so on without returning home between shows, my travel was, get this, *commuting*. How many people do you know who commute seventy thousand miles a year? How many commuters do you know who need to buy new sets of tires every six months?

This gigantic burger display must be a pain to haul around, store, and set up, but it sure is eye-catching!

Jarvis Hooten

Any reasonable person would say a road show's vehicle and travel costs are legitimate business expenses. Not the IRS. As you might imagine, driving seventy thousand miles a year and staying in hotels eight months out of twelve resulted in major expenses, all of which the IRS disallowed as business deductions. I had to pay income tax on all the money I had spent on hotel stays and fuel and maintenance for my van.

To keep the IRS off your back, minimize your vehicle, travel, and home office expense. Yes, I'm saying actually *under* report those expenses. This will clear your conscience if you choose to under report your cash sales. Make your business show a profit, even if it's just a little one, in its first year, and pay taxes on that profit. In future years, make sure you show enough profit for the IRS to believe your business is a legitimate concern.

Sales tax is much easier and less painful in most states than contending with the IRS, but it is no less important. Failing to file sales tax reports with the states where you have sales tax permits, even if you made no sales in some of those states, can result in fines, liens, and loss of your sales tax permit and business license.

To me, paying sales tax is entirely sensible and reasonable. It's a flat tax. Everyone pays the exact same amount. There is no debate over deductions or qualifying expenses. Further, sales tax is added to purchases at the time of sale. It's not a portion of a retailer's income. That's all the more reason to get those sales tax payments sent in promptly – that tax is technically never our money to begin with.

Gosh, I got off on the sour subject of the IRS just as the end of the book is drawing near. My apologies. Let's finish up with something more fun.

9 Tools Of Trade: Web Site, Cards, Stationery

So Much Digital Media, So Little Time

Once you have your first few events under your belt, it's time to make your business truly professional. You could have business cards and stationery made up before your first event, but, as I have suggested over and over, you are likely to change some things about your stand after you start doing events.

Preprinted stationery is so last century. Much more common now is to use a template in a word processing application for your letterhead. Business cards are incredibly easy to design and have printed these days.

A web site is another matter. To my way of thinking, every business ought to have a web site. I've been told my way of thinking is biased because I'm a "computer guy." That may be true, and I actually enjoy designing my own web pages, posting photos and videos from events to my "Pictures" pages and maintaining an online calendar of my event bookings. But, even if you have no computer skills at all, having a web site for your business is incredibly easy.

You don't need any of the advanced code-writing used by sites with online ordering, log-ins, databases, or java script. A vendor web page only needs a few pictures and text. Your nineteen year old niece or nephew could probably do it for you. Your web site should have a brief description of your business, a menu or product guide, and how to contact you. This could all be on one page. For the more ambitious, the site could include a calendar page, pictures page, travel blog, cooking or crafting tips, or any other fun topic you might want to share.

The cost of having your own web site has dropped amazingly over the years. In the early days of the Internet, web site hosting and domain name registration could cost hundreds of dollars a month. Now those services can be found for under ten bucks a month. There are even services that will host your site free. The drawback is, since they have to make their money somehow, no-charge hosts will use your site's pages to post advertising banners.

Once your business is established, your web site could become another source of revenue. This is especially true for merchandise vendors. Adding order forms, shopping carts, and online payment options makes a web site more complicated to design, but imagine how nice it would be to increase your sales by a few hundred bucks a month from people ordering your products on the web.

Food vendors can develop supplemental catering businesses. What a great way to maintain an income during the off season. A web site is vital for supporting and promoting a separate catering venture.

The next section is on social media, where I will state emphatically and repeatedly that you do not need to devote hours of your life to social media. However, you do need some kind of web presence. Having no Internet involvement at all these days is like not having an e-mail address or phone number. If a website seems more trouble than you care to take on, at least put up a Facebook page. Your business will not be perceived as legitimate if no one can to find you on the Internet.

Social Media

Ugh, how to tackle this one. Just hearing about social media gives me the creeps anymore. We're bombarded with reports about Facebook trends, what's happening in the "Twittersphere," who's hot on Instagram. If you're into social media, use social media; if you're not, don't. Some people swear you MUST post regularly to all social media outlets. You have to tell all your followers what you're doing and where you're going to be, all the time! Really? Do you think hundreds of Instagram followers are going to attend a festival, simply because a vendor posted a picture of their stand from the festival? Would people who aren't fans of country music attend a country music jamboree, just to visit a single vendor?

Sure, I get it, social media is fun – for folks who think social media is fun. Heck, I post pictures and videos from events to my website regularly. However, I don't expect people to come to events and visit my booth because of my website posts. My website is designed to impress event organizers, and for the fun of letting friends and family see the crazy stuff I get myself into.

If you've figured out a way to make social media marketing work for you, and you like doing it, go crazy with it! If you aren't into devoting huge chunks of your life to Tweeting, posting, commenting, and tagging, your business will grow fine without it.

Maintaining a social media presence is a part time job. The five, ten, twenty hours a week you have to commit to posting updates could be much better spent on other elements of your business. That is, unless you LIKE posting updates. If social media is your recreation, knock yourself out. But don't believe astonishing success will follow if you spend half your waking hours seeking followers. Every business does not have to Tweet or fail. Not *everyone* likes social media.

Driving in a tunnel makes it hard to see other roads. People in the social media tunnel tell us the only way to succeed is with social media. Meanwhile, only a tiny fraction of social media messages reach viewers. How many of the half *billion* Tweets posted yesterday did you read? If you could read one Tweet every five seconds, and all you did was read Tweets all day every day, you would not live live long enough to read all the Tweets posted yesterday. Don't get the jitters over Twitter. Likewise, don't fret over Facebook. How many of the 2.5 *billion* Facebook users do you follow or follow you?

Forgive me if my view on social media seems harsh. I don't despise using digital devices to connect with people, and I don't scorn people who love tweeting and tagging and posting. I'm simply fed up with the worship of social media. We're told social media is the end-all, be-all marketing tool for all businesses and professions. That simply is not true.

Social media is wonderful – for people who think social media is wonderful. Those people can use it, live their lives on it, spend half their days on it, if that's what they're into. If you love social media, you'll find ways to benefit from it. If you don't love social media, don't worry; your vending business will get along fine without it.

Mobile vending is what I call a "non-relationship" business. We don't need to chase social media followers. A customer buys something from us and goes on their way. We don't know their name, we don't create of record of their purchase history and we don't need to stay in touch with them after the sale.

After you've been in business a few years, and you've done the same events several times, you'll be delighted when repeat customers begin to seek you out. I beam with pride when people see my stand and tell their friends, "Oh good, Tropic Hut is here again. You have to try their Java Silkie!"

That's very satisfying, but, proud as it may make me feel, I'm sure no one would attend a festival solely because my Tropic Hut stand was there. It's wonderful to see repeat customers. I don't need to have them follow me online.

Relationship businesses are things like banking, real estate, advertising, and insurance. People in those businesses are perpetually networking, going to business mixers and Chamber Of Commerce functions – and desperately pursuing social media followers. They're the ones who chase followers. Did you catch the irony of that? Chasing followers?

We mobile vendors may not form relationships with our customers, but we are wise to build a network of fellow vendors and event organizers. After all, to get to our customers we have to get into events. Good relations with other vendors and event organizers get us into better events.

I send Christmas Cards to the organizers of events I work each year. Fellow vendors I've become friends with are also on my Christmas Card list, as well as in my e-mail address book. In this age of political correctness, some may not be into sending Christmas Cards. In that case, send non-religious New Year greeting cards: "Looking forward to another year of great fun and successful festivals!"

If I come across something interesting or funny I share it with my vending buddies in a group e-mail. On several occasions, fellow vendors have tipped me off to good events or recommended me to event organizers. When organizers of good festivals start *inviting* you to participate in their events, that's when you know you've arrived.

Note that none of my social interaction with event organizers or fellow vendors is expected to gain customers for my vending business. It's networking with event organizers so I can gain *access* to customers at festivals, and it's socializing with others in my field, but it's not intended or expected to reach customers directly. If that's how you use social media – you know, to socialize – your expectations are in the right place.

With that suggestion on networking we come to the close of this guide. I hope you have found a few tips that are helpful in building a successful vending business. People sometimes ask what I think are the most important factors to a mobile vendor's success. I can narrow that down to three things: products, signage, and capacity to handle rushes.

There are sure to be hurtles your business encounters that I did not cover in this book. I've tried to cover all the fundamentals, but, naturally, I can't prepare you for everything. All I hope is, every now and then as you build your business, you think to yourself, "Hey, that was a good idea!" from something you read in this book.

May your difficulties be few and your sales be many!

Vincent Cascio Photography

Jarvis Hooten

10 About The Author

My first attempt at the vending business was New Year's Day, 2005, at the Pasadena Rose Parade. Some very supportive friends worked with me to sell coffee and cinnamon rolls, hot dogs, nachos, and such. We had a great time, and it's something we'll be talking about for years, but, as a business venture, it was a disaster. In that one day I lost over a thousand dollars because of being so unaware of what I was doing.

Despite that first discouraging experience, I wanted to keep at it. I came up with an idea for a stand, spent weeks designing it, building it, and figuring out the products I would sell. My first full event with my new stand was The Run-A-Mucca Motorcycle Fest in Winnemucca, Nevada. I actually made some money and had a fun time, but I realized I was still desperately lacking in knowledge of how to make a mobile vending booth work.

You may wonder why I kept at it. Well, I could see the potential, and, in spite of the setbacks, I was really having fun with the business! Furthermore, I knew other vendors were making respectable incomes, and I was determined to figure out how they were doing it. I knuckled down and started doing extensive research on the festival vending industry.

Since those tough false starts years ago, I'm quite proud to have built up a successful business. Other vendors now routinely congratulate me on what a great looking stand I have and ask about profit margins on my inventive products. Some have suggested I go into franchising. Jees, that would be another big learning project, since I know nothing about franchising. For now I just hope this book will help others avoid my many mistakes.

After the first couple years of doing it part time, mobile vending became my full time income. I wasn't getting rich, but I did okay. Far better than the income was the satisfaction of running my own show. If you are in a job you really enjoy, where you're appreciated and surrounded by people you like being with, congratulations. You won the lottery.

Most people, regardless how wonderful their jobs are, have moments when they wish their employers didn't have so much control over their lives. Even if your job is all unicorns and fairy dust, there's bound to be at least one troll, probably your boss, whom you'd rather not spend all day with.

My last two jobs were horrible experiences. I was an Emcee/Announcer at a major casino in Reno. I had to report to and work with the most petty, vindictive, incompetent, and just plain mean people I had ever encountered. These were people I would never choose to associate with, but, since it was my job, I had to associate with them all day long.

Later I became Production Director for a local group of radio stations. The fellow who hired me was a terrific boss, but he left to take a better job. The moron who replaced him was every person's nightmare of a horrible boss. This guy couldn't pass a fifth grade literacy test, yet he strutted around as if he were the smartest guy in the building. It took all my restraint to do my job with that pinhead around, when all I wanted to do was punch him in the nose to put him in his place. How do such flaky, incompetent egomaniacs ever get into management? Perhaps you can relate.

Whether you choose mobile vending or some other venture, if you're like me, you will discover running your own business is the best way in the world to make a living. I wish you much satisfaction and success.

Made in the USA
Middletown, DE
23 May 2023

31240214R00097